Build 'Em by the Mile, Cut 'Em off by the Yard

How Henry J. Kaiser and the Rosies Helped Win World War II

Steve Gilford

Richmond Museum of History

400 Nevin Avenue

Richmond, California 94801

(510) 235-7387

All rights reserved. No part of this publication may be reproduced, stored in a retrieval system or transmitted in any form by any means, electronic, mechanical, photocopying, recording or otherwise, except brief extracts for the purpose of review, without the written permission of the publisher.

text © Richmond Museum Association Inc.

Book design by Kiersten Hanna

ISBN 978-0-6156-4873-6

Published by the Richmond Museum Association Inc. 2011

Cover Photo: Launch of *SS Robert E. Peary*, November 12, 1942. Shipyard workers assembled the Liberty ship from stem to stern in 4 days, 15 hours, and 29 minutes.

Photo, pg. iv: Shipyard workers, men and women, came from all around the country, a blend of ethnic backgrounds and ages.

FOREWORD

Congressman George Miller

This book is about a time when millions of Americans put their hearts, minds, and bodies into a clearly recognized goal, defeating the forces of Germany and Japan. The stories of the people who accomplished this are a reminder of the potential of this nation to rise up and meet a challenge. The Second World War is long over. What were once Kaiser's four Richmond shipyards now throb with different rhythms. One source is the vibrant community of Marina Bay built on the site of Yard No. 2. Another is the active Port of Richmond, increasingly a hub of international trade. And visitors to the Rosie the Riveter/World War II National Historical Park comprise the newest source. People come to see for themselves the place where innovation, dedication, and patriotism were welded together to help win the greatest war in the history of mankind.

Once again, vital challenges face us. When they seem overwhelming and when the task seems as though it might be too much for us, we can turn to the example of America's World War II home front and in particular to the Kaiser Shipyards in Richmond, California.

Taking a peaceful walk through property that was once the Kaiser Richmond Shipyards, one finds it hard to imagine that it was the site of four shipyards, where tens of thousands of workers went to and from work, with loudspeakers blaring information and entertainment to these proud laborers; where the music of brass bands and proud cheers filled the air as champagne splashed across the bows of ships slipping into the bay waters on their way to carrying America's war production and valiant military to foreign shores in this nation's war against tyranny. But it was.

Of the four yards, only Yard No. 3 remains. Remnants of its greatness are still present: the five basins where ships were created and launched; a representative whirley crane that moved huge, prefabricated sections onto the hulls; the art-deco General Warehouse that served as an air raid shelter and storage facility for the thousands of prefab parts used in construction; the employee cafeteria; a small first aid station; the machine shop; and the paint shop where metal turned battleship grey and prepared to go to sea.

Today this yard, along with the area that was home to the other three yards, has become part of the Rosie the Riveter/World War II Home Front National Historical Park. This park was established by Congress in 2000 as a memorial to the millions of Americans, all races and creeds, who mobilized to win this war. It is a place where history was made in the workforce with racial and gender integration, employee health care, and daycare for employees' children. It is a place where ships were built at an incredible pace, and where a sleepy little town of 23,000 soared to over 100,000 people in just a few short years. This is Richmond's story.

Then as now, it can be summed up as "We Can Do It!"

Editor's note: Congressman Miller was the author of the legislation conveying the SS Red Oak Victory *to the Richmond Museum Association, the only ship of the 747 built in the Richmond Kaiser Shipyards that has been preserved. He was instrumental in the establishment of the Rosie the Riveter/World War II Home Front National Historical Park. The members of the Richmond Museum Association are grateful to him for his participation in keeping one segment of this nation's history alive for future generations.*

CONTENTS

Foreword by Congressman George Miller ... v

Introduction ... ix

Prologue ... xiii

Part One: Henry J. Kaiser

An "Overnight Success" in World War II: "The Builder" ... 3

The Coming of Age of Henry Kaiser ... 7

How Henry Kaiser Came to California ... 19

Building Ships and Shipyard Simultaneously ... 25

Proud and Successful Permanentes ... 33

Ships, Steel, and Pelicans ... 37

"Call Henry Kaiser" ... 43

Fontana, California: Kaiser's Steel Mill Goes into Production ... 45

HJK's Creative Shipbuilding—The *USS Alazon Bay* ... 49

HJK and the Hatching of the Spruce Goose ... 55

June 15, 1944: Henry Kaiser on Film ... 60

Mr. Kaiser Goes to Washington ... 63

Part Two: Richmond Shipyards

Hitler Knew About Richmond ... 73

Explosive Growth, Liberty Ships, and the Poet from Oakland ... 75

The Gallant Ship *SS Stephen Hopkins* ... 81

SS Robert E. Peary: "The Wonder Ship" ... 85

The People Who Built Her ... 91

African-American Liberty Ships and the Kaiser Shipyards ... 97

The Chinese Liberty Ships … 103

The Launching of the *SS Red Oak Victory* … *107*

The Permanente Flag … 117

Christmas in the Shipyards … 118

Part Three: Rosie the Riveter

Rosie the Riveter … 125

Why Rosie Was a Welder … 145

Part Four: Kaiser Permanente

A Special Kaiser Permanente Anniversary … 153

Dr. Garfield and Dr. Kay Have Dinner at the Presidio … 155

Prelude to the Permanente Health Plan … 161

The Permanente Health Plan Begins Operation … 165

Organizing Care in the Richmond Shipyards … 173

Morris Collen Comes to Permanente … 179

The Shipyard Health Plan in Operation: 1942 … 185

Explaining Permanente … 195

Health and Safety Messages … 199

Shipyard Nurse … 203

Permanente Patient—Permanente Medicine … 207

Beatrice Lei: the First Woman Physician in the Permanente Medical Group … 210

The Permanente Health Plan Gets National Attention for the First Time … 215

Henry Kaiser's Inspiration … 220

Celebrating a Medical Center's Anniversary … 223

Acknowledgments … 229

About the Author … 231

Introduction

It started out twenty-five years ago as my simple curiosity about a place that in just a few months had been transformed from marshland on the Richmond shores of San Francisco Bay into an unprecedented giant factory for the mass production of ships—747 of them. Soon it developed into a fascination for that place and for the people there who had played a major role in winning World War II. I started by spending hours wandering all over the old yards, taking photos, and soon I was looking for the people who remembered "the old days."

I had been fortunate to have had the opportunity to study history with three outstanding scholars: in high school, Russell Ayres, and later at Yale the prominent historians Thomas Mendenhall and Alois Nagler. (I was not the only person inspired by Mr. Ayres. Among his students were Adlai Stevenson and John F. Kennedy.) I owe a great deal to these three teachers. At a time when the predominating attitude of historians was to dismiss this approach as anecdotal, they each had emphasized the value of appreciating the individual's perspective of great events. In their classrooms, such stories had made history come alive for me. Twenty-five years later, wandering through the nearly abandoned shipyards, I wondered about the lives of the people who once filled these acres with their accomplishments. I began searching for them and writing down their stories.

My road to the Richmond, California, shipyards has certainly not been direct. You might even say that it ran through the Kaiser Permanente Medical Care Program. It began in the television studios of New York and Washington, D.C., where I spent more than twenty years as a PBS television producer/writer of national documentaries specializing in science, medicine, and health care. Between broadcast documentaries, I directed and produced continuing medical education programs for the National Institutes of Health and had my first introduction to the innovative, prepaid group practice, Kaiser Permanente.

Until 1983, being on the East Coast, I had very little contact with Kaiser Permanente. However, I spent most of that year in California working on a special children's science series to inaugurate the Disney Channel. When the series was completed, like so many before me, I decided to remain in the Golden State. I was able to find periodic contract work with Kaiser Permanente and took the opportunity to learn more about its principles and its history. That's how I was introduced to two intriguing figures at the center of that history, the founders of Kaiser Permanente. One was Henry Kaiser, the larger-than-life industrialist who had helped shape the modern American West. The second was the lesser-known Dr. Sidney Roy Garfield.

Garfield has been cited as one of the one hundred most influential physicians of the twentieth century. He discovered the potential of prepaid group practice to provide affordable, high-quality care through a system that turned the economics of medicine upside down and prospered by keeping people well, rather than relying on sickness and injury for income. Kaiser and Garfield had first put these principles into operation during the building of Grand Coulee Dam. Here, Kaiser was also forging a group of experienced builders who would later bring their know-how as organizers and builders into the shipyards and would transform an entire industry. Garfield would develop a health care program for the shipyard workers that would, as historian Kevin Starr later wrote, "Kaiser [Permanente] is the great big social idea to come out of World War II."

Although I have never been an employee of Kaiser Permanente, the relationship between the development of this book and Kaiser Permanente has been a close one. The support I received from many people over the past several decades, especially Kaiser Pioneers, has made this book possible. Jack Chapman first intrigued me with his reminiscences of working side-by-side with founders Henry Kaiser and Dr. Sidney Garfield. Permanente Medical Group founders Cecil Cutting, M.D. and Morrie Collen, M.D. shared their recollections of the wartime period in the shipyards. My early efforts at collecting Kaiser history were supported by Bob Bodine of the Kaiser Permanente Audiovisual Department and then increasingly by Sharon Levine, M.D. and Holly Ruehlin of the Permanente Medical Group. For the past several years, support has also come from Tom Debley, himself a historian, author, and now retired director of the Kaiser Heritage Resources Department (where I act as senior history consultant), and his successor, Bryan Culp.

Now that the site of the former shipyards has been officially recognized as the Rosie the Riveter/World II Home Front National Historical Park, I am particularly pleased to have found and interviewed the undoubted (although unrecognized) original Rosie the Riveter, an eighteen-year-old recent high school graduate working at the Sikorsky aircraft plant in Bridgeport, Connecticut. For what may well be the first time, I have been able to fit her firsthand story into the tale of how Rosie the Riveter became a national icon, how the nickname developed from a casual phrase in a gossip column into a slogan that still resonates nearly seventy years later.

Appropriately, hers is just one of the stories that make up this book, history from the point of view of the men and women who came together to build ships faster and better than had ever been done before and who helped win a world war. Over the years, I've written many articles on Henry J. Kaiser and each of his endeavors, in particular the shipyard years and the birth of his revolutionary health plan. The stories in this book are some of my favorites, culled from my years of collecting Kaiser home front information and most especially from having gotten to know the people who made some of this history happen.*

I have interviewed scores of people in the fast-thinning ranks of former shipyard employees: welders, riggers, chippers, naval architects, shipyard executives, sweepers, even a shipyard translator, as well as the men who took these Richmond ships into every one of the world's oceans. In New York State I visited the Kaiser boyhood home in Canajoharie and heard family stories about the Kaisers there. I followed Kaiser's trail to the site of his first business in Lake Placid (where as a photographer he achieved his first success). As my interest increased, I visited World War II shipyards from Maine to California and the iron mine and the steel mill that provided the plate for building ships. The stories that make up this book are ones that I learned from the people in those places. It is history from the point of view of those who lived it.

Steve Gilford

---

* I have altered some of the original articles to avoid redundancy, but some duplication necessarily still exists.

Prologue

The attack on Pearl Harbor did not, in itself, galvanize America into the kind of home front mobilization most people associate with the United States during World War II. The surprise attack by Japan in late 1941, however, did unleash an overwhelming anger and indignation toward that nation. People were amazed that a small island country on the other side of the Pacific should have the foolhardiness to make a sneak assault on American bases without even a declaration of war.

At first, there was little immediate appreciation for the military might of the Japanese Empire. Most people assumed that Japan could be defeated rather easily; a few bombers over Tokyo would be enough to set their wood and rice paper houses on fire. That would destroy the Japanese will to wage war. At first, the federal government, for both military and political reasons, tried to shield the American public from the reality of the situation—from how much damage had been done to the American Army and Navy forces in the attack and how powerful the Japanese military had become.

Ambrose Bierce, writer and satirist, almost a century before had said, "War is God's way of teaching Americans geography." His cynical statement was proving true in December, January, and February as news flowed in from unfamiliar locations such as Bataan, Corregidor, Wake Island, and Midway. Americans learned how important these places were for safeguarding supplies of industrial staples such as raw rubber and crude oil. Thousands flocked to bookstores to buy maps so that they could follow the news from these faraway places with the strange sounding names. Talk of shortages and even rationing began to be heard. It started to seem that civilians, too, were going to have to make sacrifices.

The "good" news during this period was not of victories, but of "gallant holding actions" and "orderly withdrawals in the face of overwhelming enemy strength." The first heroes were the subjects of inspiring stories; the courageous survivors of ship sinkings and soldiers determined, at the risk of their own lives, to make the Japanese pay heavily for every scrap of land they took.

Around this time the account of the actions of one chaplain at Pearl Harbor made its way to the newspapers of the day. He had been in the midst of delivering a sermon on a battleship in Pearl Harbor that Sunday morning when his ship was attacked. He grabbed a helmet and manned an anti-aircraft gun, crying what became a catch phrase of the period, "Praise the Lord and pass the ammunition!!"

In Europe, the situation was no better than in the Pacific. The U.S. ally Great Britain stood alone. The Nazis ruled Poland, Czechoslovakia, Holland, and Belgium. In North Africa, the Afrika Korps' tank divisions, commanded by Erwin Rommel, "the Desert Fox," were sweeping across the desert landscape, with only minor setbacks, threatening the Suez Canal and Egypt, which was the gateway to the rich oil reserves of the Middle East. Across the English Channel from Occupied France, Great Britain now faced an invasion by the German army massing along the French coast. German submarines were sinking her supplies on their way from factories and farms in the United States, supplies that she so desperately needed in order to keep fighting.

With a diet of news like this, it began to dawn on politicians and the general public that the United States might very well be in a fight for survival.

The February 23, 1942, issue of *Time* magazine called the previous seven days "the worst week in American history in this century," with "one great trip hammer blow after another." The issue was filled with recent news of convoy sinkings, retreats, and defeats around the world. By any standard, this was a national emergency, and by the end of February 1942, the whole nation knew it.

Part One
Henry J. Kaiser

THE BRIDGE BUILDER
Will Allen Dromgoole

An old man going a lone highway,
Came, at the evening, cold and grey,
To a chasm vast and deep and wide.
The old man crossed in the twilight dim,
The sullen stream had no fear for him;
But he turned when safe on the other side
And built a bridge to span the tide.

"Old man," said a fellow pilgrim near,
"You are wasting your strength with building here;
Your journey will end with the ending day,
You never again will pass this way;
You've crossed the chasm, deep and wide,
Why build this bridge at evening tide?"

The builder lifted his old, gray head;
"Good friend, in the path I have come," he said,
"There followed after me today
A youth whose feet must pass this way.
This chasm that has been as naught to me
To that fair-haired youth may a pitfall be;
He, too, must cross in the twilight dim;
Good friend, I am building this bridge for him!"

When Kaiser died in 1967, this poem was read as a part of his funeral service.

Previous Page: Henry J. Kaiser

An "Overnight Success" in World War II:
"The Builder"

If in 1941 you asked the proverbial "Man on the Street" who Henry Kaiser was, there's a pretty good chance your answer would have been a blank stare. Most people, especially away from the West Coast, wouldn't even have recognized the name. Within the next year, though, 1942, Henry J. Kaiser became one of the best-known and most-admired men in America. After the humiliation of Pearl Harbor, the nation needed heroes, and Kaiser filled that need. His very real accomplishments took on an almost legendary quality as the millions of readers of such magazines as *Life*, *Time*, *Look*, and *The Saturday Evening Post* discovered this "wonder man." In a nation where the most popular form of public entertainment was the movies, HJK was a regular feature of the weekly newsreels that ran before the main films. His shipyards were "turning out ships by the mile and cutting them off by the yard." When his suppliers could not supply him with enough engines for his ships, and it looked as though he might be slowed down in his production of the badly needed vessels, he went into steam engine building himself. He needed more steel, so he built a plant. The public could not seem to get enough Henry Kaiser stories. His Permanente Cement Plant was supplying material for rebuilding the damaged military facilities in Hawaii while other Kaiser plants were manufacturing munitions and a variety of other things needed by the armed forces. When he gave a speech at the launching of a ship, there were always network radio microphones there to carry the Kaiser enthusiasm and confidence out to the nation. Henry Kaiser was a larger-than-life maverick. He constantly challenged the accepted ways of doing things, and the results always seemed to be "More, Better, and Faster" than anyone had thought to be possible. It is no surprise, that with this sort of exposure and popularity, in three years he would be a serious candidate for the vice-presidency of the United States.

To much of America, the man seemed to have exploded onto the national scene, an "overnight success," but as is usually the case with overnight successes, he'd been preparing for it for many years. When you look back at Henry Kaiser's remarkable career, it seems as though the previous twenty-five years had been careful preparation for the role he would play in World War II. Henry Kaiser himself gave the best explanation of how between 1914 and 1941 he turned a small street paving company in Vancouver, British Columbia, into one of the most valuable wartime production assets of the United States: "… you can't get fine talent into your organization by simply offering high salaries. You and the men who work with you have to build yourselves up to the capacity to tackle bigger and bigger jobs." The twenty-six years were spent building, step-by-step, the skills, capital, and confidence that it would take to manage a workforce of 300,000 during World War II.

The source of Henry Kaiser's enthusiasm and energy was that deep down, he did not consider himself to be a manufacturer, a contractor, or even an industrialist. He was sincerely committed to something of much more value—he was a Builder. To him, building was one of the noblest of human activities. His favorite poem was Will Allen Dromgoole's "The Bridge Builder." He thought it expressed his feelings so well that when he was called to testify before a Congressional committee about wartime production, he asked for the opportunity to recite this poem to the committee members. Luckily, the unusual scene of one of the most powerful men in America, in a deep rumbling voice, reciting poetry to a Congressional committee, has survived on newsreel footage. Separated by more than a half-century, transmitted by film with a scratchy sound track, Henry Kaiser still has the ability to inspire. In the last stanza, the old gray-haired builder's answer to the traveler's question of why he builds clearly had great meaning for Henry Kaiser, who at the outbreak of World War II was nearly sixty years old. He was building not just for the present, but also for generations to come.

Henry Kaiser visiting one of his ships under construction at the Richmond Shipyards.

Just one month before the U.S. government accepted the finished Boulder Dam project, two years and two months ahead of schedule, HJK and his partners posed proudly in front of their "impossible" creation: (left to right) Harry Morrision, HJK, Frank Crow (job superintendent), Felix Kahn, Guy Stevick, Gus Ayers, and Steve Bechtel.

The Coming of Age of Henry Kaiser

On December 4, 1942, at a gathering of America's most powerful and influential business leaders held in the ballroom of New York's Waldorf-Astoria Hotel, Henry Kaiser delivered a remarkable speech. In twenty-odd minutes, Kaiser, who had only in the past year achieved public acclaim for having revolutionized shipbuilding methods, showed he was evolving into a unique combination of businessman and statesman, admired and trusted by the public at large. A few days before the first anniversary of the attack on Pearl Harbor, while U.S. forces were fighting against the armed forces of Imperial Japan in the Pacific and Rommel's Afrika Korps in North Africa, Henry Kaiser chose for his topic, "Management Looks at the Post-War World." America's role in World War II was just beginning, but Henry Kaiser was already looking well into the future. His speech was carried live on network radio, and Kaiser used the opportunity to set out his goals. He had recently told a journalist: "I'm not kidding myself about this present crest of the wave. Today people on the street spot me as if I was some movie actor. I'm riding the wave, but it won't be long before it hits the rocks. But by God, while I'm up on the crest, I am going to start things; I'm going to try to get a few things done." His speech that day was filled with compassion, humanity, and vision. In a sense, Kaiser had been preparing that speech for his entire life, but it was in the months leading up to that night that his vision as well as his "voice"—the way he presented that vision—took final shape.

Henry Kaiser's Mission

One of the most amazing things about the astonishingly varied career of Henry Kaiser is that he did not really hit his stride until he was sixty years old. Already known and respected within his profession at the outbreak of World War II, Henry Kaiser was not yet a public figure. His vision was broad enough to see how the great public works projects he had directed—the tunnels, bridges, pipelines, and especially the giant dams—were changing the American West. It was World War II that provided him with extraordinary opportunities on a national level, especially shipbuilding, and he seized them. Within a few months, the success of his shipyards had transformed him into one of the best-known and most-trusted men in America. He had begun to carve a unique place for himself in the American consciousness as something never seen before: an industrialist-statesman.

As a contractor and businessman, Kaiser had been very successful during the 1920s and even in the Depression years that followed. The two-hundred-mile highway his men had built down the center of Cuba, across mountains and through pestilential swamps, had shown what his organization could accomplish under the most difficult circumstances. It had also made him a millionaire. Even so, few people outside of the construction industry appreciated the magnitude of what he and his company had accomplished in Cuba or the abilities of the organization he was building. The Permanente Cement Plant that he'd started in 1938 was huge, modern and efficient, and growing rapidly, but again, it was essentially a regional activity. The dams—Hoover, Bonneville, and the biggest of them all, Grand Coulee—were impressive, but they, too, were more regional than national in impact, and Kaiser shared the success there with his Six Companies partners. One of them, though, Warren "Dad" Bechtel, had taken a liking to the younger man and had become a kind of mentor to him. He had encouraged Kaiser to think nationally, and when Bechtel stepped down as president of the Associated General Contractors of America (AGC), Henry Kaiser was elected to succeed him. As AGC president, Kaiser had become spokesman for the industry on government and labor issues. The position also gave him the chance to hone his skills dealing with the federal government and to develop contacts that would later prove very useful. He remained focused on the interests of his company and of his profession. But the time was coming when he would speak to, and for, the nation.

Sidney Garfield, the physician-founder of Kaiser Permanente, had seen a hint of what was to come, when in 1938, at Grand Coulee Dam, he first met the builder and had a chance to explain how prepayment could shape a successful industrial health care program. Kaiser had grasped the concept and the implications immediately. Garfield remembered him saying: "Young man, if your idea is half as good as you say it is, it's not only good for this project, it's good for the entire country." Kaiser had made a leap from the specific of a medical care program for his workers to the general, a nationwide, industrial-based health plan, reasoning that such a good idea should not be confined to Kaiser projects. Something within the contractor seemed to be resonating to the larger societal goal.

Perhaps this shift had something to do with Kaiser's growing interest in religion. HJK had become friendly with one of his neighbors at Lake Tahoe, where he had built a vacation home. The Rt. Reverend Noel Porter, Episcopal Bishop of Sacramento, was minister at Cathedral in the Pines, a simple outdoor chapel just down the road from the Kaiser home. Kaiser had started attending church on a regular basis when he was at Tahoe. It hadn't been long after HJK's conversation with Dr. Garfield at Grand Coulee that the builder had been confirmed in the Episcopal faith by his friend Bishop Porter. He had already begun to take an active role in the church's affairs and had been invited to give lay sermons from the pulpit. His later public addresses had some of the characteristics of a sermon as he began to link his ideas to social issues and to present them in moral and ethical terms.

By fall 1942, Kaiser's organization was fully immersed in wartime production. His shipyards were launching ships faster than anyone had ever done before. His steel plant, which had been the site of orchards and pig farms just a half-year earlier, would begin producing massive amounts of steel for the war effort in only a few months; that steel would speed up production in his shipyards even more. Meanwhile, Kaiser engineers were working on two promising methods of meeting the nation's need for the strategic metal, magnesium. He was also busy building Navy fighter planes, and manufacturing artillery munitions, and new projects seemed to keep coming up.

Where once there had been pigs, there was now a steady supply of pig iron. It only took Henry Kaiser and his crews nine months to transform what had once been pig farms and orchards into a steel mill providing a new source of that desperately needed metal for shipbuilding and other wartime uses.

A continuing stream of favorable mentions of Kaiser's achievements in newspapers, radio broadcasts, and newsreels had turned him into a celebrity, but he had not immediately understood the opportunities that came with this new status. That began to change in July 1942. At the launching of one of his Liberty ships at Portland-Vancouver, Kaiser proposed a radical new approach to the challenge of delivering the vitally-needed millions of tons of war materiel that were pouring out of home-front factories to battlefields on the other side of the world's oceans. To the astonishment of a national radio audience, he proposed a fleet of 5,000 giant air freighters, seaplanes twice as large as anything then in the air. By retooling his shipyards, he promised he could deliver these planes in eighteen months. The German submarine blockade would be broken as aerial convoys of these seventy-ton giants flew high above the U-boats.

Perhaps understandably, established aircraft builders were very uncomfortable with the idea of Kaiser entering the aircraft field. After all, only a few months before, he had been a neophyte shipbuilder, and now he was setting production standards in shipbuilding for even the old-line companies. What might this industrial maverick do to the aircraft industry if he started building planes? The planemakers lobbied the legislators to convince them that such gargantuan aircraft were a pipe dream and that to divert scarce resources to try to build them would be a setback to the war effort.

Unexpectedly, the public, excited by the simplicity and scope of his vision and well aware, thanks to admiring journalists, that Kaiser had already achieved many things "experts" had told him were impossible, provided enthusiastic support for the air freighter idea. Newspaper and radio editorials applauded the concept. Public opinion forced the government, albeit reluctantly, to offer Kaiser a contract to develop the plane. Design of the air freighter, in cooperation with Howard Hughes, went forward, and Kaiser had learned something of the value of public opinion in getting his ideas implemented.

While managing a workforce approaching 300,000 people fully committed to wartime efforts, Kaiser devoted his formidable excess energy to planning for the postwar period. In early September 1942, the *Oakland Tribune* reported on a Kaiser speech in which the optimistic industrialist took on the gloomy predictions of those economists who held the pessimistic position that the war's end would bring the return of the Depression as war industries closed down and millions of soldiers came home looking for jobs. Kaiser saw postwar America quite differently and predicted that "a pent-up consumer demand will be released." He was sure that the end of the war could bring unprecedented prosperity for the American nation, if the country was willing to prepare for it. Production, not retrenchment, was the key. He argued that the billions of dollars Americans had put into savings through war bonds would fuel this postwar boom. They would pay for hundreds of thousands of new homes, household appliances, cars, and the scores of luxuries that had disappeared during the war. There would be a need for new roads and new transportation systems, and technologies developed during the war would be the basis for whole new industries. America, if properly prepared, could produce its way to new levels of prosperity.

Although not alone in this kind of forward thinking, Kaiser was in the minority. He was disappointed that more of his colleagues in American boardrooms did not share his point of view and that they seemed to be approaching the postwar period with a caution that he felt could damage the nation's chances of returning to prosperity.

Kaiser had found his mission but he hadn't yet found his voice, the way he would present his vision to the nation. However, in the next few weeks, he would.

Henry Kaiser Finds his Voice

Although Henry Kaiser was not well known before he began building ships in 1941, his very public successes confounded the so-called experts. By fall 1942, Kaiser's shipyards had first set a world's shipbuilding speed record and had then smashed that record by half. Then, only weeks later, they had cut the record by more than half again, to an astounding four-and-a-half days from laying the keel to launching. HJK's achievements started appearing first in the *Saturday Evening Post* and then in *Life*, *Time*, *Fortune*, and other magazines. At a time of military uncertainty, these stories raved not just about HJK's shipbuilding accomplishments, but also of his earlier achievements: how the "impossible" Hoover and Grand Coulee dams were built ahead of schedule and under budget, and how, when he had lost out on the bidding to construct Shasta Dam, he more than made up for it by bravely plunging into the cement business, breaking up the West Coast cement monopoly, and winning the huge contract to supply the millions of tons needed to build that great dam at a reduced cost to government.

America was still reeling from the effects of Pearl Harbor and needed heroes. "Hurry Up Henry" caught America's imagination. For millions of people, his unorthodox methods and "can do" attitude represented the best in the American spirit—energy, ingenuity, hard work, and optimism. His idea of replacing the fleets of merchant ships with a trans-Atlantic bridge of air freighters high above enemy submarines only added to his public reputation. Were such planes feasible? He was willing to stake his company and his reputation that they were.

Each new magazine article led to invitations to give more speeches—to rally the home front, to sell war bonds, and to express a sense of purpose for America's worldwide struggle. From Kaiser's wartime speeches, it is clear, even from the darkest beginnings, that he never doubted the Allies would ultimately win the war. By fall 1942, he was convinced that how the victors handled the peace would be every bit as important as how they waged the war, so in late September, when he was invited to join a prestigious list of international speakers that included several governors, a platoon of generals, and several presidents of major corporations, as well as many leading politicians and diplomats, to address the *New York Herald Tribune's* Annual Forum, he knew what he wanted to talk about. It was not about how the United States must rally to win the war—he took victory for granted. Instead he said, "It may be difficult to focus attention on any phase of the war other than victory. Notwithstanding, there are factors no less important than the destruction of Rommel's army, and the domination of the South Seas. Indeed, America's most difficult task at this hour may be to employ her spiritual and intellectual capacities so as to understand what this war means, and to fully comprehend the import of its consequences."

Kaiser added, "For is it not a fact that we could win the war with arms, and lose it by economic, political and social blindness?" That is what had happened after World War I, and mistakes made at that time had helped lead the world into a second global conflict within a generation. Now, less than a year after America's entry into World War II, Henry Kaiser was already thinking about how to avoid postwar pitfalls that might lead the world to another war in ten or fifteen years. He picked up on the theme of his earlier address in Oakland that peace does not have to mean a return to the conditions of the Depression. For him, the key was freedom.

The preceding January, President Roosevelt had outlined "Five Freedoms" that are the bedrock of human rights around the world: the Freedoms of Speech, Religion, and Information and the Freedoms from Want and from Fear.[*] Kaiser wanted to add one more freedom. This one, he believed, was the engine that could drive the new society.

---

[*] President Roosevelt originally spoke of five freedoms at a press conference at Hyde Park, July 5, 1940. Six months later, in his much more public declaration of his thinking, he had dropped the freedom of information; it was from this second iteration that artist Norman Rockwell took inspiration and created the "Four Feedoms" series of covers for the *Saturday Evening Post* published in 1943.

> *[I] suggest that we add another freedom to the five enumerated by our President: the Freedom to Produce. I am aware that there is a suggestion of materialism about this proposal, and that there are those who will stoutly proclaim that there is no hope for the future. …*
>
> *[But] without abundant and profitable production our institutions of learning could not be sustained, nor could the life-giving research within and without these institutions be pursued. Without the means to train and develop scientists, engineers, physicians, technicians, organizers and managers, our civilization would collapse.*

According to Henry Kaiser's view, the country could produce its way to prosperity. All that was needed was the will to do so.

By late 1942, Kaiser was beginning to shape a more comprehensive view of the postwar world. It was that view he presented when he returned to the Waldorf-Astoria, on December 4, 1942, to address the National Association of Manufacturers (NAM). He had been invited to speak because of his growing reputation for accomplishment and also to share his outspoken optimism. The NAM organizers, in those early days of the war, wanted someone who could provide their members with an uplifting message. Speaking before some of the most powerful people in the country and with his words being carried coast-to-coast on radio, Kaiser reached out with the ideas he had been formulating for America's future.

He believed deeply, as a matter of faith, that the country's future was in free enterprise, not in a centrally-planned economy. Competition in the marketplace would lead the world to prosperity. As for the great postwar economic boom he had spoken of earlier, he now had some specific examples, "four avenues of opportunity, in no sense exclusive, but wholly typical of the type of activity which could quickly generate an immense volume of employment."

Housing:

HJK had recently read a report of a national survey of real-estate professionals predicting a postwar need for 9,000,000 housing units. To him this meant the need for millions of jobs, not just in construction, but in all of the related activities ranging from lumbering to manufacturing and selling the household appliances and furnishings for these new homes.

Transportation:

After several years with no civilian automobiles being manufactured, there would be a gigantic pent-up need for new cars. Building, selling, and servicing them could provide hundreds of thousands more jobs. The potential was enormous. Although he did not mention it, Kaiser was already investigating this market for his own postwar activities.

Highways:

Kaiser wasn't the first to suggest a national network of highways—World War I hero, General John "Black Jack" Pershing had done that in 1922—but HJK had been a road builder and knew the social and economic value of good highways. The recently-opened Pennsylvania Turnpike and the Merritt Parkway in Connecticut helped him form a vision of a safe, beautiful, national highway system linking markets and encouraging leisure travel. He suggested to his audience that this giant public works project would be an investment in the future that would pay off handsomely. This was nearly fourteen years before the birth of the Interstate System.

Health care:

It was probably on the subject of health care that Henry Kaiser was most outspoken that evening. He had seen the difference it had made in the productivity and morale of his work force at Grand Coulee Dam. He also knew how well it was working in his shipyards already served by three hospitals: the Field Hospital (also called the Richmond Field Hospital), Fabiola (also called Permanente Hospital), and the Northwest Permanente at his Columbia River shipyards. Perhaps more to the point, over the past four years, he had had the opportunity for long talks with Sidney Garfield, who had progressed from being his industrial medicine consultant to becoming a personal friend. Dr. Garfield had described to Kaiser the system he and his colleague Dr. Raymond Kay had begun planning: industry-based medical centers in communities across the nation. They would be self-sustaining and operate on a prepaid basis. Their physicians could organize into multi-specialty group practices. The doctors' plans had been derailed by the war, but Kaiser recognized the power of the concept, and from his "bully pulpit" in the Waldorf-Astoria ballroom that evening, he threw out a challenge that carried Garfield's and Kay's ideas out to the nation:

> *Will the manufacturers now dare to organize, finance, and manage medical centers in every industrial community, where medical service could be purchased on an insurance basis at a cost which would bring not only skilled facilities but all the advantages of research within the reach of the common man, and at the same time provide the doctors of America with a participation which would adequately remunerate them for their long and expensive training?*

In Kaiser's mind, organizing health care not only made sense, it was the right thing to do for American society.

Perhaps it was the influence of his friend from the Cathedral in the Pines at Lake

Tahoe, the Rt. Rev. Noel Porter, that caused him to present his thinking in what reads almost like an old-fashioned sermon mixed with visions of a bright future filled with amazing electronic devices and even atomic power. He spoke of "the eternal truth that Nature's laws are his [Man's] servants, if he will have the spiritual competence to employ them." He even quoted Scripture to the business leaders, "Be ye doers of the word and not hearers only," and presented a modern parable to encourage his audience to not only listen to what he had to say but also to take action. Although many present that evening resented being told what they ought to be planning in their own industries and brushed off his "Johnny-come-lately" ideas, a recording of that speech has survived, and Kaiser's obvious sincerity comes through the sometimes florid and bombastic phrases.

Perhaps that sincerity reached out more successfully to ordinary Americans than it did to the audience seated before him that night. Requests for copies of the speech poured in from radio listeners. Certainly President Franklin Roosevelt recognized that there was something extraordinary about this colossus out of the West who could organize armies of workers in huge projects, who could create and innovate on a grand scale and who could articulate an inspiring vision of a socially equitable America that was powerful and possible.

Less than a year and a half later, Henry Kaiser would find himself at the President's home in Hyde Park, being evaluated as a possible running mate for FDR. For reasons that probably had more to do with politics than FDR's personal preference, Harry Truman ultimately received the nomination. However, Kaiser's serious consideration as a candidate did point out that Henry Kaiser had evolved into something new in America: a businessman with a statesman's view of the world who believed that the way to do well was to do good.

How Henry Kaiser Came to California

A major reason why San Francisco's East Bay became the site for four Kaiser shipyards is that Henry Kaiser loved Oakland. He had moved there for sound business reasons, but he very quickly came to love the city. Years later when his operations had grown so much that he had to keep offices in New York's Rockefeller Center as well as in Washington, D.C., there were those on his staff who thought it would make more sense for him to be located there, closer to the sources of money and power. However, he would have none of it. Even when the Kaiser "empire" spread across the entire globe, onto every one of the inhabited continents, the Kaiser World Headquarters remained in Oakland. The story of how it happened that HJK moved the successful Kaiser Paving Company down to California from the state of Washington is almost mythic in the way it sums up the energy and determination of HJK, qualities that could also be seen in his vigorous and enthusiastic approach to shipbuilding.

In the late teens and early 1920s, the Kaiser company had been very busy. It had been bidding successfully on one contract after another in the Pacific Northwest, taking advantage of a frenzy of road building as the nation created an infrastructure of paved roads to support the fleets of new vehicles pouring out of America's car and truck factories. Alonzo B. Ordway, Kaiser's right-hand man, had been working non-stop for several years, helping the young company become established as a major road-building firm. Finally, he'd been able to take a vacation.

"Ord" and his wife had driven down to Northern California for a restful week away from the paving and road construction business. On their way home, while having dinner in Redding, a small Northern California city, Ordway overheard two local contractors discussing a soon-to-be-awarded contract for the thirty-mile stretch of road between Redding and Red Bluff that today is part of Route 99.

When Ordway heard the contractors say that this job could be worth more than a half-million dollars, he started paying close attention. Knowing "The Boss" was always eager to hear about big highway jobs coming up for bid, he made sure the next morning to send him a telegram containing all the information he had been able to garner. Then he and Mrs. Ordway left town, driving north toward home.

That evening, the couple found accommodations for the night at one of the finer hotels in Portland, Oregon. As they were registering, Ord was amazed to find a message from HJK waiting for him. Kaiser, knowing the direction Ord was driving, had reasoned that since he was traveling with his wife he'd be staying that night in one of the more comfortable hotels in Portland. He had simply sent messages to all of them!

What Kaiser's telegram said was that he had decided to go after the Redding-Red Bluff highway contract. The telegram also carried the news that HJK was at that very moment en route to Portland from Washington State to meet Ordway and that the two of them would go directly to the town of Redding and submit their bid. However, it had to be done quickly. There was a deadline, and it was the next day.

The following morning, as Mrs. Ordway continued home, driving the family car alone, the two men went to the Portland railroad station and caught the Shasta Special south toward Redding. It was then that they learned they had a problem. Ordway later recalled, "After we boarded the train, we discovered that the train didn't stop in Redding!"

However, in those days before radios, necessary communication to the engineers about the conditions ahead and information to coordinate the movement of trains sharing the same sections of track was done by sending telegraph messages to stations along the line. The messages, called "train orders," would be placed on a pole outside the telegraph office alongside the track. As the train passed through, the engineer would slow down enough so that he could snatch his orders from the end of the pole. Ordway learned the Shasta Special would be slowing down to pick up orders as it passed through the Cottonwood station, about sixteen miles south of Redding.

Soon Ordway was afraid he'd made a mistake telling the forty-year old Kaiser about the slow-down. Kaiser now figured that if they could somehow get off the train in Cottonwood they could get transportation to take them sixteen miles back to Redding.

> *He decided to grab his suitcase and jump. We went up to the middle of the train where there wasn't any brakeman and we opened the vestibule to jump off. I used to do a little hobo-ing in my time and was pretty good at hopping off moving cars but Henry was a little heavy and we both had suitcases.*
>
> *He let go near the little Cottonwood station house and tumbled head over heels, skidding head first into a pile of railroad ties. . . . The station master came out just as we got to our feet and were examining our skinned hands and legs. "You damned fools," he said, and, of course, he was right. We lost a little skin and ruined our suits but we did get the job at $527,000, our biggest up to then, and we've been in California ever since.*

Whenever he told the story, "Ord" always smiled as he recalled the look on the station master's face as the portly Henry Kaiser tumbled across the train platform in a cloud of dust.

Henry and Bess Kaiser with Alonzo B. Ordway, Kaiser's "right-hand" man, at the banquet held after the launch of the SS Honduras Victory, *July 7, 1944.*

It seems only right that with that sort of initiative Kaiser would win the contract. He did, and it turned out to be a major turning point in his career. At the time, the record for highway construction in California was a half-mile per week. With a combination of careful planning, innovative, efficient and creative use of equipment, and a talent for building an organization whose workers took pride in the speed and quality of their work, Kaiser was soon building road at twice the old record. Before the Redding-Red Bluff job was finished, Kaiser had constructed a reputation in California for excellence and dependability.

After his success on the Redding-Red Bluff job, Kaiser had no trouble finding more California jobs for his crews. The state was in the middle of paving thousands of miles of dirt roads. The potential for additional work for someone with his proven record was enormous. HJK moved his headquarters to Oakland to be closer to his expanding activities in the Golden State.

For the rest of their lives, both Ordway and Kaiser enjoyed telling the story of their arrival in California—torn, tattered, and ready to do business. In the shipyards and for decades beyond, how they had rolled into Cottonwood had become a part of Kaiser Company lore. Their adventure symbolized the "Can Do" attitude of the Kaiser workforce—people who set record after record building more ships faster than anyone else in history.

How Henry J. Kaiser and the Rosies Helped Win World War II

One of the most delicate jobs in the shipyards was the lifting of the prefabricated sections of the deckhouses, weighing as much as seventy tons. It meant keeping the load carefully balanced between the four cranes needed to make the lift and setting it down on the precise spot where it would be welded to the hull.

Building Ships and Shipyard *Simultaneously*

In July 1940, the British Merchant Shipbuilding Mission arrived in the United States with $96,000,000 in cash looking for someone to build ships for them. They wanted sixty ocean-going freighters of what would be called "Ocean Class" vessels.

Although World War II was raging in Europe, the United States was not yet directly involved. Great Britain, an island nation, was being starved into submission by fleets of German submarines that were sinking the freighters supplying desperately needed food and armaments far faster than new ships could be built to replace them. So successful were the U-boats, that this period of the war became known to German

On January 13, 1942, construciton began on Yard No. 3 at the Richmond Shipyards. This time, instead of filling in marshland (as they had done previously), Kaiser engineers created new land by cutting back Brooks Point, a small mountain that ran down to the Richmond shore.

submariners as "Die Glückliche Zeit," "the Happy Time." In his postwar memoirs, the man who led Britain through this perilous period, Winston Churchill, wrote, "The only thing that ever really frightened me during the war was the U-boat peril." It was clear that without new ships to keep supplying her with food and arms, England could not hold out against the Germans much longer. Something had to be done.

How Henry J. Kaiser and the Rosies Helped Win World War II

What the British Mission found was that the United States had already stepped up its own shipbuilding program, and there were nowhere near enough vacant shipways left to accommodate such a huge order. Despite the fact that Henry Kaiser and his organization had no experience building ships and had no shipways, HJK recognized this as a business opportunity. It was a remarkable feat of salesmanship for Kaiser to land a contract to build thirty of those freighters at a yet-to-be-constructed shipyard on the shores of San Francisco Bay. According to Kaiser company lore, their executives, on the way to Washington to meet with the British Mission, stopped off in New York to visit the public library and take out books on shipbuilding to prepare for submitting a proposal!

Throughout his career, Henry Kaiser was always able to make skillful use of partners already expert in a field he wished to enter. He had done it in construction; he would do it in automobile manufacturing and in several other of his major ventures. This time he joined with W.S. "Pete" Newell of the Todd Shipbuilding Company. He had already worked with the Todd Company on a number of projects including the conversion of two ships to bulk carriers of Permanente cement.

Todd Shipbuilding was a good choice for a partnership. Todd, operating on the East, West, and Gulf coasts, was one of the country's most experienced shipbuilders. Bath Iron Works, owned by Todd and located in Portland, Maine, had been building ships since their founding in the 1880s. (They had even built a battleship, the *USS Georgia*, launched in 1904.) Todd and Kaiser would split the British contract between them. The Todd Company would build thirty of the British Ocean Class vessels in their East Coast yards and Kaiser, with the Todd Company as his partner, would produce thirty ships in California. Cyril Thompson, the leader of the British Mission and son of the designer of the Ocean Class vessels, remained in the U.S. for several months to help the Kaiser people in the planning of their new shipyard in Richmond, California.*

Building a Shipyard

Within a month of signing the contract to construct thirty ships, Kaiser crews began building the first of what would ultimately be seven West Coast shipyards. Henry Kaiser didn't have many shipbuilders on his construction crews, but up on the Columbia River at Coulee Dam he had been building something that was perhaps more significant—an innovative executive team and a loyal, efficient workforce. As the Coulee project was nearing an end, Kaiser began moving men and equipment down to Richmond as rapidly as possible. The transferred crews went to work building the shipyard and ship with the same spirit that had helped them finish that "impossible" dam across the Columbia River, years ahead of schedule and under budget.

For ten thousand years, the harbor shore that came to be called Richmond, California, had provided food for bands of Ohlone Indians who camped there, just above the shoreline. More than ten millennia of discarded shells, remains of countless sea-given meals, had actually lifted some areas into what are called shell mounds. However, most of the land along the shore remained flat, soft, and marshy. By the twentieth century, this land was regarded as nearly worthless except by young East Bay children who would grow up remembering with great fondness the hours they spent fishing and exploring that great salt marsh.

---
* On his way back to England, Thompson's ship was torpedoed. He spent nine hours at the oars of a lifeboat before he and the other passengers were rescued.

How Henry J. Kaiser and the Rosies Helped Win World War II   27

With the war in Europe and thirty ships needing to be built, work began that was going to turn the isolated marsh into one of the great production battlefields of a war that the United States had not yet decided to enter.

In 1940, the rainy season began early. The rain was unrelenting that morning when Otis H. McCoon, a Kaiser foreman, who had been with Henry Kaiser at Grand Coulee, ordered the first tractor out into the quagmire to cut a service road from Cutting Boulevard down toward the shore. McCoon and the others soon had a gloomy glimpse of what it was going to be like to build a shipyard there. The tractor sank out of sight into the marsh! Not only were they going to build a shipyard; first they were going to have to create eighty acres of solid ground to build it on.

With their experience at Grand Coulee, Bonneville, and Hoover Dams, as well as the two-hundred-mile highway in Cuba and countless other construction projects, Kaiser and his crews were past masters at earthmoving. Experienced engineers estimated that firming up the land would take six months. Instead, "Hurry Up Henry's" crews, working 24-hour shifts that were to become the Kaiser wartime norm, finished the job in three weeks, and work began on the shipyard that was to become Richmond Yard No. 1.

The architect of the yard, responsible for designing the scores of buildings that would be needed, was Maury Wortman. Wortman soon found himself running the equivalent of a large architectural firm, but he still had difficulty keeping up with the construction crews. At times during the building of the ship-

Maury Wortman, chief architect of the Kaiser Richmond Shipyards. Wortman was responsible for the design of scores of buildings and shipways, including the impressive cement warehouse still a feature of Yard No. 3.

ways, the workers got ahead of the architectural drawings. However, Wortman seems to have handled the job with skill and diplomacy, because after the war he was hired to design hospitals for the Kaiser medical care program, among them the Redwood City, Santa Clara, and Bellflower medical centers. His prize-winning design for a medical office building in Antioch earned him national notice.

While writing this article and trying to think of a way to give some perspective to the stunning achievement begun back then, I took a break to go through my mail. It was January, and I realized that in only a few months I would have to file my tax return. Then it struck me. Between then and that looming deadline of April 15, in that same space of time, Kaiser's crews would have built a shipyard, literally from the ground up. And within those same few short months, by April 14, 1941, they had been able to lay the keel of the first of 747 ships to be built in Richmond. Adding to that achievement, while construction in Richmond was running full tilt, other Kaiser crews were busy on the Columbia River, building the first of three Kaiser shipyards in the Northwest. Those yards were to turn out an almost equal number of ships. Henry Kaiser had started on his way to eclipse Helen of Troy. After all, her face launched only a thousand ships.

Kaiser Builds His First Ship: the Ocean Vanguard

As a ship design, Ocean Vanguard had a past that stretched back well into the nineteenth century. The British shipyards of J.L. Thompson and Sons had been producing ships built on this basic plan ever since they had launched the first one in 1879. Slow but dependable, the Thompson-designed-and-built tramp steamers were a familiar sight on every trade route of the world's oceans. Their technology was old but they were dependable, sturdy, and simple to build.

Ocean Vanguard *just after launching, August 16, 1941. In peacetime America, the launching of a ship was an attraction for a small fleet of pleasure craft to assemble offshore from the shipyard. The object of their attention was the* SS Ocean Vanguard, *Henry Kaiser's first ship. The ship still needs much more work at the outfitting dock before it will take on the more familiar look of a completed ocean-going freighter.*

As obsolete as the Ocean Class ships may have appeared to the ship designers of 1940, it was a brilliant design for the needs of the time. The hull was angular, without graceful compound curves, which meant that the hull plates were easy to shape. The design was also very adaptable to the new electric arc welding techniques and needed less of the slower and more expensive riveting process. The ship's engines, of a simple, proven design, operated under comparatively low steam pressure. These were much easier to produce in the large numbers required than were the far more powerful steam-turbine engines that were currently being installed in U.S. warships (and would later power the Victory ships). The ship had a single deckhouse, making it easier to build and reducing the need for costly and time-consuming wiring and plumbing, thereby shortening construction time even more. The Ocean Class freighter was a perfect design with which a new shipyard could gain experience. More complex ship designs could come later.

As the yard was built around her, the new ship rose in the ways. Remarkably, the *Ocean Vanguard* was ready for the water in just four months. On August 15, 1941 Kaiser's first ship slipped down the ways and into San Francisco Bay. She was ugly, awkward, and old-fashioned. She was not even an American ship. What the *Ocean*

Vanguard was, though, was one of the most significant ships ever built. Her design would have an astonishing future. She would be the model for Liberty ships, and more Liberty ships would be launched than any design in maritime history.

By the time Kaiser finished the thirty-ship contract for the British Merchant Shipbuilding Mission, he was nearly a half year ahead of schedule.

Sometimes shipyard workers had to learn to live with bitter disappointment when the results of all their efforts went to the ocean bottom. On September 13, 1942, the *Ocean Vanguard* was torpedoed by the German submarine U-515, 70 miles east of the island of Trinidad, and sank with the loss of eleven lives.

The *Ocean Venture*, another of the thirty vessels Kaiser built under the British contract, also met an unfortunate end as a victim of a German submarine. Today she is well known to sport-diving, amateur archaeologists. A recent eyewitness report described what can be seen today:

> *One of the most visually spectacular wrecks off Virginia, the* Ocean Venture *was a 7,174-ton freighter sunk in 160 feet after being torpedoed by the U 108 on February 8, 1942. . . . From the large engine, one can follow shaft alley to the stern, large lead ingots on either side. The wreck has greatly fallen apart. The stern proper is listing to port with the remainder of stern structure scattered around the sand. The bridge is upside-down just off of the port side. The helm, telegraph, numerous portholes, and many other artifacts have been recovered. The* Venture *still has numerous loose portholes throughout the wreck, though most are contorted from multiple depth charges subsequent to the sinking. Due to its distance offshore, the* Venture *can have incredible visibility. (Retrieved from www. Wreckdive.com May 11, 2011.)*

How Henry J. Kaiser and the Rosies Helped Win World War II   **31**

Gate at Kaiser Richmond Shipyard No. 2.

Proud and Successful *Permanentes*

For several decades, the name "Permanente" was associated more with successful commercial innovation than with medical care. Its use began in 1939 when Henry Kaiser bid successfully for the contract to supply cement needed for building Shasta Dam in Northern California. At the time, he had never produced a single bag of cement and he didn't yet have a plant in which to produce cement. In record time though, he had built a plant, located in the hills south of San Francisco, and put it into operation. He named his new company Permanente, after a very attractive stream that flowed year around through a canyon on this property, both in the rainy season and during Northern California's dry summers. The product was known as Kaiser's Permanente Cement. This was the first time the names "Kaiser" and "Permanente" were joined.

Because Henry and Bess Kaiser liked the sound and the associations of this Spanish word for "permanent," it seemed natural that when HJK needed a name for the new company that would operate his first two shipyards in Richmond, California, he used the name there, too: the Permanente Metals Company. (While Shipyards No. 1 and No. 2 were under the direction of Permanente Metals, Shipyards No. 3 and No. 4 were operated by Kaiser Cargo.)

Not well known is the fact that when Kaiser went into the shipbuilding business, he already was a ship owner. In 1939, in addition to his cement plant, he founded another Permanente organization, the Permanente Steamship Company, to sail between California and Hawaii.

The Permanente Steamship line, though, was not for passengers, it was for cement. At that time, cement was loaded onto ships in one-hundred-pound bags stacked on palettes. Palettes were lifted from the docks into the air by cranes and cargo booms and lowered into the cargo holds, where longshoremen heaved the bags around into place, stacking them in an orderly arrangement. It took days to load thousands of tons of cement into a moderate-sized freighter and as ship operators are fond of repeating, "a ship doesn't make money tied up at the dock." Loading and unloading was a labor-intensive, time-consuming, and therefore expensive, part of the cement business.

Construction of the Permanente Cement Plant began in June 1939, and by Christmas of that year, it had produced its first cement. Soon "Hurry Up Henry" was operating one of the largest cement plants in the United States.

Kaiser reasoned that if his company could just pour bulk cement into a ship's hold without the bags and unload it using pneumatic hoses to blow it into storage

containers on shore, it would save a great deal of money. It would allow him to make a profit on Permanente cement from California sold in Hawaii. He could open up a whole new market.

Experts scoffed. They told him that during the time at sea, the cement would absorb moisture and the powdery material would harden leaving him with a ship filled with a useless cargo. However, Kaiser's own people had looked at the idea, and he was convinced it would work. The next step was to find some ships.

In October 1940, HJK found two that met his needs. The *SS Phillipa* and the *SS Ancon* were being sold by the Panama Canal Company, which no longer had any use for them. The *Ancon* became the flagship of Henry Kaiser's small fleet. He renamed her *SS Permancnte*.

The *Permanente*, built almost forty years earlier, already had an interesting history. At the grand opening of the Panama Canal in 1914, the first ship to make the historic trip from one ocean to the other through the new canal was the *Ancon*. Just three years later, during World War I, the U.S. government temporarily commandeered her to transport troops across the Atlantic. Now as the *Permanente* she was going to carry cement.

Before Kaiser could put the two ships into service, they needed to be remodeled into bulk carriers. Kaiser had his modest flotilla towed to Seattle where the Todd Shipyards Company put them into dry dock and prepared them for their new role.

When the first shipment of cement arrived in Hawaii in a Permanente ship, Kaiser was proven right. Not only was the new technique for transporting the cement a great commercial success, the two ships turned out to be a significant national wartime asset. The *Permanente* and the *Phillipa* set records delivering cement across the Pacific to where the U.S. Navy's construction battalion, the Sea Bees, used it to construct harbors, airfields, and military bases for U.S. forces as they advanced from island to island towards Japan. But that wasn't the most significant outcome of Kaiser's seagoing cement.

Even more important to the war effort than the accomplishments of the Permanente Steamship Company was that the outfitting of the Permanente ships had been done at the Todd Shipyards in Seattle. While the ships were being worked on there, Kaiser met the company's dynamic president, John Reilly.

The Todd Company was an old established shipbuilding firm with roots reaching well back into the nineteenth century. The two men agreed that there was about to be a boom in shipbuilding, but Reilly lacked the men and equipment he needed to take advantage of it, while Kaiser had no experience in the field. What Kaiser could offer, though, was an experienced, skilled, and highly-motivated workforce fresh from its success at Grand Coulee Dam, as well as much of the heavy equipment that would be needed. For his part, John Reilly headed a company with years of shipbuilding experience as well as an excellent reputation.

The "seadogs" and the "sandhogs" formed the partnership that won the British contract for the freighters and brought Kaiser into the business of ship construction. Soon, though, Kaiser would choose to be on his own. New approaches to ship construction developed in the Permanente Metals shipyards and the five other yards Kaiser operated would set standards that even veteran shipbuilding firms would have to live up to.

Ships, Steel, and Pelicans

"Whenever Henry Kaiser enters a business, it is not long before his head is bumping the ceiling."

By 1942, Henry Kaiser stood at the head of an organization made up of people who, from top to bottom, thought that they could tackle any project, enter any industry, and do it better than anyone else had ever done before. If you questioned them about it, you would be likely to get an answer back that sounded like, "That's no brag, Mister, just fact!" They had good reasons for that attitude. They could remind you that just a few years before, Kaiser had led his workers into the dam-building business, and soon they had been building not just the biggest, most difficult dams in the world, they were completing them under budget, ahead of a tight timetable, and with a healthy profit.

They could point to the time when Kaiser had decided to open a cement plant. It had been built within a year and Kaiser had become a major figure in that industry, too. Then he had turned to shipbuilding. Within months, by building shipyards and simultaneously beginning a revolution in the way ships were built, he had become a major player in that field, also.

When he had forecast a steel shortage in the West, he grappled with the established steel producers "back east" who wanted to keep him out of their industry. He also had to convince a reluctant government to give him permission to turn some pig farms and orchards in Fontana, California, into a giant steel mill able to take iron ore in one end and turn out steel plates and beams from the other. He built that plant from the ground up, and before the year was over, his crews had been producing Kaiser steel, using ore from a Kaiser mine. The steel would be used to build the Liberty ships, Victory ships, tankers, aircraft carriers, and troop transports that would be coming out of his shipyards.

In September 1942, Kaiser's business associates gave him a testimonial dinner held at the Scottish Rite Auditorium in Oakland to celebrate his massive achievements of the previous year. In the speech he gave that night he said, "the fundamental assumption is that there is nothing that reasonable men undertake which cannot be accomplished." It was a cornerstone of his beliefs.

After Pearl Harbor, the press discovered that Henry Kaiser could help fill the public's need for wartime heroes. As big as they were, the Kaiser companies didn't yet have a public relations department. It was the press that sought Henry Kaiser. The Kaiser stories, as they were told in magazine articles, newspaper features, and in the newsreels run before the main feature in movie houses across the country, were all basically the same—a version of the Horatio Alger rags-to-riches myth.

Henry Kaiser really did fit the Horatio Alger model, at least in some ways. He was the son of immigrants and while growing up in a small town he had dreamed big. He had gone to the city and, through intelligence, daring, hard work, and honesty, became fabulously successful. Young Henry may not have been penniless, but he did start as a sales clerk in a hardware store where for a full week's work he was paid $1.50. Even in 1895 dollars, that was very little money. He had to walk the four miles to work in the morning and four miles back in the evening just because he could not afford trolley fare.

Like an Alger hero, he had great energy. He did not seem to have a personal work schedule, he just worked. He started with small successes and built on them.

Birthplace of Henry J. Kaiser, circa 1885. Henry was born in the village of Spout Brook (in 1882), in the township of Canajohairie, New York. According to the present owner of the house, the future industrialist and builder was born on the second floor in the rear room whose window we can see in this photograph. The woman in the foreground is unidentified.

Somehow along the way, he learned how to recognize opportunity and had the courage to make the most of it. Each business venture was more successful than the previous. With the coming of World War II, in order to get done what he knew needed to be accomplished, he sometimes had to go to battle against his own government's bureaucracy. All of this just increased public admiration for the man who now seemed to stand like a Colossus, tools in hand, ready to take revenge on America's enemies.

However, not everyone saw Henry Kaiser the same way. A number of the industrial and financial leaders of the time explained his success differently. They claimed Kaiser was a product of "government handouts." After all, he wasn't succeeding in a normal market. In this wartime emergency, when government contracts were flooding out of Washington, he might be doing well, but when normal times returned and there were no longer huge defense contracts, they wondered aloud, "How would this Johnny-come-lately do then?"

Kaiser was a religious man and sometimes his speeches sounded a bit as though he were delivering a sermon. It's not hard to imagine that he was a bit miffed at any downplaying of the accomplishments of "his boys" as well as himself. In that speech he gave before the National Association of Manufacturers, about three months after the testimonial dinner in Oakland, he told the leaders of industry gathered there that night a parable that contained his answer about succeeding in the postwar world. It was the story of a band of pelicans living in California's Monterey Bay.

> *They had been living very comfortably on the refuse from a busy sardine cannery in the bay, but the fishery had been over-harvested and now the factory had to shut down. A whole generation of pelicans had grown up knowing nothing else but the reliable bounty of the sardine factory, and now it was over. The young pelicans grew upset. They protested. But when they found that their protests were doing nothing to solve their problems, they turned to their elders. They wanted to know how the pelicans had survived before the cannery. They were ready to listen to the voices of experience. The oldest pelican spoke. "There is only one answer to your need for food—you must fish for it."*

Kaiser believed that when the country went back to a peacetime economy, industry had to be prepared to compete in a free market. He had no doubt that he and "his boys" would be ready.

Working for *the Boss*

*Henry Kaiser with shipyard workers.
Clearly HJK was comfortable with the workers and they with him.*

In 1990, when William Soule, a junior executive in HJK's Oakland office during World War II, was asked why people drove themselves so hard for "the Boss" he answered:

"to be able to play for a savvy coach who would inspire them to win games. You got on the team and fought 'over your head.' If you made a mistake, the coach went through the incident over and over until you both knew the problem and the likely answer. And you tried again.

"For me, in June 1941, this was a challenge I could not refuse. I was drawn to it as a moth to a lighted candle. Fortunately, when I came into that cone of light I was not consumed by the flame. Singed, perhaps, but not consumed. It was a scary, exhausting, altogether exhilarating experience."

If you want some big construction, and the speediest production - do away with all obstruction,
Call Henry Kaiser!
If you want to build a byway or a subway or a highway - or even build a skyway,
Call Henry Kaiser!
He'll tackle a job that others give up, and make it fast and stronger.
But if the job's impossible, it takes a little longer.
He'll build a dam or a fountain, he's a man that you can count on if you want to move a mountain
Call Henry Kaiser, Go on, Call Henry Kaiser!

"Call Henry Kaiser"

I felt very fortunate to get a tour of what two decades earlier had been a major Kaiser Center exhibit honoring the one-hundredth birthday of Henry Kaiser. My "tour leader" was the late Gene Trefethen, formerly Chief Operating Officer of Kaiser Industries as well as a lifelong friend of HJK. When the exhibition closed, in 1993, Trefethen had it moved to a barn at his winery in Napa, where he sometimes could be persuaded to show it to people with a special interest in Henry Kaiser. While at the winery doing some work for "Mr. T.," I asked if I could see the exhibit. He volunteered to take me through it himself.

I looked at all sorts of fascinating materials representing the worldwide achievements of the more than one hundred Kaiser companies. One modest item that caught my eye was a piece of sheet music entitled "Call Henry Kaiser." The pages had been mounted on a board so it was impossible to read the full music score. What I really wanted was to hear how the music sounded. Recently I found a recording. More than sixty years ago, "Call Henry Kaiser" had been performed by the Harmonettes as part of a network radio drama, a biography of HJK, sponsored by Mutual of Omaha. I managed to locate a 78-rpm vinyl transcription of the program[*]

In the photo at left, Henry Kaiser, his wife Bess, and Clay Bedford (general manager of the Richmond Shipyards, second from right) pose with the Harmonettes, a singing group made up of women working in the Richmond yards. Their recording of "Call Henry Kaiser" played on national radio. The photograph was taken at the launching of the USS Missoula, a Richmond Victory ship built for naval use, September 6, 1944.

---

[*]Sheet music from the archives of Kaiser Permanente Historical Resources Department.

At Henry Kaiser's insistence, his steel plant at Fontana, California was not only productive, it was also attractively landscaped with lawns and fruit trees.

Two days after this first plate steel was rolled at Kaiser's new Fontana plant, it had made the 450-mile trip from Fontana, Caliornia to the Richmond shipyards and became part of the SS Emma Lazarus at her launching. The tiny cartoon figure hanging on the rear, holding onto the reins, is the Fontana mascot, Snorty, the pig.

Fontana, California:
Kaiser's Steel Mill Goes into Production[*]

By late 1943, some of Henry Kaiser's less charitable competitors were calling him a publicity-seeking show-off. Kaiser's success in a variety of fields, shipbuilding in particular, was making some established leaders in those fields very nervous, and now he was entering the steel business. In late 1942, when his steel mill at Fontana was about to go into production, Kaiser's industrial accomplishments were the subject of a steady flow of admiring feature stories in newspapers, newsreels, magazines, and on the radio. His astonishing success as a shipbuilder had already caught the imagination of the nation, and the stories about him featured not just current achievements but also his previous projects. Some, such as the Hoover, Bonneville, and Grand Coulee Dams had helped to reignite the American "can-do" spirit that had been severely dampened by the Great Depression. Now Americans were learning that "Hurry Up Henry" had been one of the major forces behind those jobs. What stood out in all the stories was his ability to blast through the bureaucratic entanglements that seemed to be threatening to strangle the nation's war effort, a talent the country needed.

Although Kaiser had not yet felt the need to open a full-fledged public relations department, he had already learned that being an admired public figure helped his workers build a sense of pride in themselves. After all, he was being admired for their

---

[*] Much of the information in this article comes directly from the Kaiser Steel employee newspaper, *The Snorter*, the weekly eight-page publication produced for Kaiser employees at Fontana. In securing this resource, I had the help of the well-known Kaiser collector in Pennsylvania, David Antram, who is also president of a national association of Kaiser automobile owners and who continues to be a great source of information on a variety of Kaiser topics.

achievements, and he never let them forget that he appreciated it. This acknowledgement seemed to sharpen their desire to take on new and bigger challenges. For instance, in April 1942, when his crews had begun construction of a steel mill on the site of a pig farm in Fontana, he announced that "his boys" would have a blast furnace in operation before New Year's Day. And if that wasn't enough, four months after that, he promised, they would also have a rolling mill there, turning Fontana steel into plates for hulls of the Liberty ships so badly needed for the war effort.

There were plenty of people who were convinced, however, that this time Henry Kaiser had bragged himself into a corner. No one had ever built a steel plant that fast, and Kaiser had the additional handicap of wartime shortages of some of the materials he had to have to build his plant. It was hard to find anyone in the steel business, except Kaiser and his crews, who thought the Kaiser schedule was anywhere near possible. However, at two o'clock on the afternoon of December 30, one day ahead of her husband's self-imposed time limit, Bess Kaiser threw the main switch that lit the fires deep inside in the 1,200-ton blast furnace her sentimental spouse had named for her.

Because Kaiser had raised nationwide interest in the race to get his steel mill into operation by the end of the year, the opening ceremonies were covered by the major news organizations of the day. The Columbia Broadcasting System (CBS Radio) broadcast the proceedings across the country while newsreel cameramen recorded the event to be shown the following week in movie theaters in every part of the country.

In the same way that veteran politicians say "all politics is local," Henry Kaiser believed that all production was local. He knew how to transform even the biggest business event into a family affair. Dedication Day for the blast furnace he had named Bess was a good example of this. His younger son, Henry Jr., was the Master of

Ceremonies, and his older son, Edgar, took time off from running the Columbia River shipyards to attend the ceremony. Just as there was always a sponsor to christen each ship launched at Kaiser's shipyards, Bess Kaiser became the sponsor of her ten-story-high, 130-foot-around namesake.

Entertainment for the occasion was drawn from the Kaiser "family," too, and featured "The Singing Sentinels," a quartet of talented security guards from the Kaiser Oregon Shipbuilding Company. The guards, who often entertained at ship launchings, had already gained a following there. Standing on the platform in front of that gigantic blast furnace named "for the Boss's wife," they sang the sentimental love song, "Let Me Call You Sweetheart," a favorite of Mr. and Mrs. Kaiser.

The Kaisers sincerely thought of their employees as an extended family, so they were all invited to the dedication ceremonies. These were the men who, once again, had done a job that many had said was impossible. They deserved to take some precious time off to enjoy their accomplishment; so, after eight months of unrelenting 'round-the-clock labor, work came to a standstill for several hours. In another nationally broadcast speech, Henry Kaiser credited these people with having accomplished this construction job faster than almost anyone other than he and they had believed possible.

For the same reasons that HJK, with the help of Dr. Sidney Garfield, had created a health plan for the nearly 200,000 shipyard workers, he introduced a similar program for the employees of the Fontana plant. It was the beginning of a relationship with the town of Fontana that continues today. It also marked the beginning of what would become the Southern California Region and the Southern California Permanente Medical Group.

While under construction, the first of the Kaiser carriers was called Alazon Bay *but at the last minute, her name was changed to the* USS Casablanca, *celebrating the recent successful Allied landings in Morocco and the war planning meeting (known as the Casablanca Conference) between FDR and Great Britain's Prime Minister Winston Churchill.*

HJK's Creative Shipbuilding:
The USS Alazon Bay

One of Henry Kaiser's outstanding characteristics was what we call today "thinking outside the box." On April 5, 1943, at Kaiser's Vancouver shipyards, First Lady Eleanor Roosevelt smashed a bottle of domestic champagne across the bow of a new aircraft carrier and christened it the *USS Alazon Bay*. The ship was another of Henry Kaiser's unconventional ideas. Even in a life filled with highlights, the satisfaction of the launching of the *Alazon Bay* must have stood out.

A year before, the Allies were clearly losing the war, due in large part to German U-boats operating close to the U.S. coast. Crowds on beaches in New Jersey and in Massachusetts sometimes watched helplessly as a tanker or freighter exploded and burned in the night a few miles offshore. The Germans were sinking ships faster than Allied shipyards could replace them.

Although the number of U-boat sinkings was kept out of the public press, Henry Kaiser was well aware how serious the situation was becoming. He knew there had to be a better strategy than just increasing the number of ships being built in the hope that more would get through. Kaiser came up with three interesting possibilities.

He explored the idea of building helicopters capable of operating from the deck of merchant ships. They could patrol the waters around convoys, looking for submarines and could lead sub-hunting surface ships in for the kill. However, even Henry Kaiser, "The Great I Can," as he was called in contemporary newspaper articles, had to admit that helicopter technology was not yet up to the challenge.

Another possibility was to build giant flying boats to carry war materiel far above the periscopes of the German wolf-packs. For a while, Kaiser promoted this idea tirelessly, pushing reluctant bureaucrats in Washington to supply him with the authority he needed to begin work building a fleet of these airships. Production problems, however, proved to be far more complicated than anyone had forecast. Howard Hughes took over the project, but before the "Spruce Goose," the first and only one of these planes to be built, had made its one brief flight, the war was over.

It was his third idea, though, that turned out to be a big winner. It was another way of providing air cover for endangered convoys. One of the best defenses for a convoy was aircraft patrolling the sea lanes ahead of the ships. Submarines caught cruising on the surface were extremely vulnerable. Under favorable circumstances, even submerged submarines could be spotted from the air and bombed. Allied aircraft flew protective missions from land bases east and west, but the planes' ranges were limited. In mid-ocean there was an "air gap," a very dangerous part of the crossing. Aircraft carriers that could travel with the convoys could help fill that gap. Although large aircraft carriers were proving to be the most valuable ships in the Navy, there were too few of them. They were expensive, and they took well over a year to build. Kaiser was convinced that his shipyards could produce a smaller aircraft carrier in great numbers. These General Purpose, GP, or "Jeep," carriers could escort convoys and find and sink submarines from the air. His naval architects designed a carrier, little more than half the size of the big fleet carriers, that could be built on a modified version of the ship's hull Kaiser shipyards were already turning out. Kaiser was sure he could produce each scaled-down carrier in a matter of weeks.

When he tried to set up a meeting with Navy Department officials to tell them about his small carrier design, they were less than eager to hear his ideas. They seemed annoyed that a civilian would presume to design a warship. Kaiser put on the pressure, using all his influence to get a hearing. When it became clear to the Navy that ignoring Kaiser was not an option, an impressive group of brass, including four admirals and the U.S. Navy's chief naval designer, agreed to meet with him in Washington. Quickly, clearly and enthusiastically, Kaiser explained to the group how these versatile ships were not meant for battle but could provide much-needed protection for convoys. They could also be used to ferry new aircraft to battle zones and to provide air cover for invasion troops. Far less expensive and less complicated than full-size carriers, the Navy could have a lot of them—quickly. Kaiser promised that six months after he began production, he would be able to launch thirty of the little carriers. Kaiser finished his presentation with a promise to handle what was one of the Navy's biggest problems: "Okay this ship and I'll lick the submarines."

The admirals considered Kaiser's proposal briefly, and then they voted. The count was a disappointing sixteen to zero against it! The meeting from beginning to end had taken eighteen minutes.

There are two old sayings: "Fortune favors the prepared mind" and "Fortune favors the bold." Either could explain what happened next.

Kaiser and his Washington aide, Chad Calhoun, were walking back from that brief and unsuccessful session with the admirals when they ran into an acquaintance of Calhoun's. Mordecai Ezekiel was also a friend and advisor to President Franklin Roosevelt. Standing on the city sidewalk, the three men began talking about the proposed aircraft carriers. When Ezekiel showed interest in the idea, Kaiser unrolled his engineering drawings. In a city park, on their hands and knees, the three went over the design while Kaiser explained the advantages of the concept. Ezekiel was so impressed with the idea that he thought it should be brought to the attention of the President himself. He knew the President admired Kaiser, so he felt he could set up a meeting between the two. He told Kaiser and Calhoun to stand by and be ready to come to the While House on short notice. The call came the next morning.

When Kaiser and Calhoun were ushered into the Oval Office, they were surprised to see that the President had also invited several of the same admirals who just the day before had turned down the idea of "baby carriers." Kaiser resisted the temptation to gloat over his new opportunity to present his idea and just went ahead with no more than his customary enthusiasm.

Earlier in his career, Franklin Roosevelt had served as Assistant Secretary of the Navy, and he quickly understood the potential of this new class of aircraft carrier, even if his admirals did not. Now Commander-in-Chief, he did not take a vote; instead, he "requested" that the Navy arrange for Kaiser to produce one hundred of what they were now calling "escort carriers," CVEs, to differentiate them from the big "fleet carriers." The Navy, still not convinced of the value of the little carriers, was later able to have the order cut back to fifty, and fifty were built.

And how did the fifty little carriers perform?

They lived up to HJK's predictions. They ferried hundreds, if not thousands of fighter planes to the battle areas where they were needed. Other planes flying off their decks helped clear the Atlantic of German submarines. They also brought added firepower to American island invasions across the Pacific. Even though not designed for combat, in the Battle of Leyte Gulf, their planes helped a small naval force drive off a much larger and more powerful Japanese fleet attempting a counterattack on vulnerable American forces recently landed in the Philippines. Their task force fought so aggressively that the Japanese admiral thought he had run into the U.S. main fleet and retreated.

Winston Churchill, who once said that the only thing that had really frightened him during World War II was the success of the German submarines, told Henry Kaiser, "Your escort carriers turned the tide of the submarine war." The Navy brass changed their minds, too, and on the one-hundredth anniversary of Henry Kaiser's birth, in appreciation for HJK's contribution to the war effort, they launched the *USNS Henry J. Kaiser*, the first of eighteen Kaiser Class ships. Kaiser Class ships are fleet oilers. Fittingly, these are the ships that carry the fuel that makes it possible for naval warships to do their jobs by replenishing their stores at sea.

The Spruce Goose on the shore in Long Beach, California being prepared for what would be her only flight on November 2, 1947, one mile, at an altitude of 70 feet over the harbor, at a speed of 135 miles per hour.

HJK and the Hatching of the *Spruce Goose*

In 2005, millions of people around the world watched the Oscar awards. The film with the most nominations, including "Best Picture," "Best Director," "Best Actor," "Best Supporting Actor," and "Best Supporting Actress," was the Howard Hughes biography, *The Aviator*. Although the name "Kaiser" does come up once in the film, few of the millions who watched the Oscars that night realized that there were strong Kaiser connections to the real-life Howard Hughes and to events dramatized in the film. One of them is the project most often associated with Hughes, the giant seaplane, the HK-1, better known as the Spruce Goose.

An adjective often used to describe Henry Kaiser is "impulsive." From time to time, when he became very enthusiastic or very frustrated, he was known to "shoot from the hip." Sometimes the results were spectacular. In the summer of 1942, Kaiser was becoming increasingly frustrated, and in a sense it was his own fault.

By continually refining production techniques, the Kaiser shipyards were launching Liberty ships in an average of forty-nine construction days, an almost unbelievable ninety-four days ahead of the schedule set up by the U.S. Maritime Commission. What this meant was that the Kaiser shipyards were consuming steel and other hard-to-get raw materials far faster than anyone had foreseen. The resulting shortages were slowing down the output of ships from the Kaiser yards in Richmond and up along the Columbia River. "Hurry Up Henry" certainly did not like that. Then

HJK heard that the Maritime Commission had diverted scarce supplies he had been counting on for his yards to another shipyard. He was furious. Meanwhile, during the previous week, German U-boats had sent 100,000 tons of urgently needed ships to the ocean bottom. Kaiser had to agree with U.S. Navy Admiral Emory Land, head of the Maritime Commission, who said that the American shipbuilding program, even with all its successes, was like trying to put out a fire by throwing more fuel on it. Kaiser decided to come up with an alternative.

By 1942, Henry Kaiser had become something nearly unique in American life: a businessman with a popular following. When he gave a speech he received national coverage. On July 19, 1942, HJK's speech in Portland, Oregon, at the launching of the Liberty ship *Harvey W. Scott*,* was carried live on network radio all around the country. This was no ordinary "we thank all the people who made this ship possible" kind of speech. With the help of Palmer Hoyt, publisher of Portland's influential newspaper, *The Oregonian*, and a strong supporter of the aircraft industry, Kaiser had prepared a surprise.

He began with a recital of shipping losses due to enemy action, a staggering 400 ships in the Western Atlantic in the seven months since America had entered the war. Kaiser then sprang his surprise—a dramatic proposal to use his shipyards to build a fleet of giant airplanes. He said, "Our engineers have plans on the drafting boards for gigantic flying ships beyond anything Jules Verne could have imagined." Once again Kaiser was thinking big. He told the nation that if he got the go-ahead from the government for the necessary materials, he could build 5,000 huge seaplanes of a size that would dwarf anything that had ever been built to fly before. These cargo ships of

---

*Harvey W. Scott (1838-1910) in 1863 became the first person to receive a baccalaureate degree from Pacific University—one of the first degrees awarded in the western United States. He went on to become editor of *The Oregonian*.

the air would be able to cross the Atlantic in a matter of hours, high above the German submarine wolf packs.

HJK's associates, the young men on his management team who would have to carry out "The Boss's" grand scheme, were stunned. They had never even heard of this proposal until it came through their radios that Sunday afternoon.

Kaiser's idea rapidly took on a life of its own. The national wire services picked up the story. Soon, Henry Kaiser's flying freighters were being promoted in newspapers across the country and even abroad, and radio newscasters were congratulating him on his vision. During the next weeks, magazines ran stories about this proposed new flying marvel with artists' imaginative renditions of what they thought the Kaiser plane would look like.

Something about the enthusiasm of HJK and the directness of his solution to the terrible submarine losses had caught the imagination of press, politicians, and the public. People began writing their congressmen, telling them to get government out of the way and let Kaiser loose. Government war planners had been caught flat-footed by Kaiser's audacious proposal.

The Navy had listened to the industrialist's suggestion, but, perhaps feeling threatened by the shift from sea to sky, came to a different conclusion. It decided that the "Super-Cargo Plane" was impractical. Furthermore, it argued that diversion of vitally-needed workers and materiel away from the construction of tankers and freighters needed to supply Great Britain, the Soviet Union, and our troops in the Pacific would only damage the war effort. The Navy also asked: "What did Kaiser know about building airplanes?"

However, there was soon so much political and popular support for the Kaiser idea that the government could not ignore it. Forced into a compromise, they awarded

HJK a contract, but not for the 5,000 of these gigantic flying boats he had proposed. Instead, they authorized him to build only three. Established aircraft manufacturers were dismayed to see Kaiser entering their field, realizing that if he entered the aircraft industry, he would be a powerful postwar competitor. They encouraged the government to further hamstring the industrialist by denying him access to scarce materials such as lightweight metal alloys he needed to build the planes.

Kaiser was undeterred. First he began looking for a collaborator with experience building aircraft. He had done this when entering other new fields, such as shipbuilding, and more recently, steel manufacturing. He had found collaboration helpful, at least to get started. This time he found a partner who was as well known as himself—movie producer, aircraft designer, and record-setting pilot, Howard Hughes.

Together, they planned the giant airship which was to be called the HK-1 (Hughes Kaiser-1). It would be six times larger than any aircraft of the time. Everything about it would need to be gargantuan—the wings would be longer than a football field. And if the government wouldn't let them have the necessary metals they needed to build this colossal aircraft, they would build it out of wood! (Even though it would be made primarily of birch, it became known by a name Hughes disliked, the Spruce Goose.) To counter charges that the HK-1 would be taking skilled aircraft builders away from military aircraft assembly lines where they were needed, woodworkers from around the country were recruited. The revolutionary new airship body was to be constructed by people, many of whose previous experience had been making furniture!

Unfortunately, perhaps predictably, the Kaiser-Hughes partnership soon foundered. Problems designing a plane this size powered by eight of the largest aircraft engines ever built, capable of carrying 750 soldiers or two battle tanks across an ocean, were far more difficult than either man had anticipated. The plane dropped way behind schedule and rose high above budget. Furthermore, HJK had trouble dealing with Hughes' work style. When it became obvious that it would be years before the first of these planes took to the air, Kaiser's attention moved on to new enthusiasms.

Now without Kaiser, Hughes kept working on the HK-1. Finally, on November 2, 1947, with Hughes at the controls of what was expected to be a routine engine test, the Spruce Goose accelerated to 75 knots and rose 75 feet above the slightly choppy waters of Long Beach Harbor. The builder-pilot held the plane there for almost a minute before he set her gently back on the bay. It was the first and last flight of the only airship of the giant fleet envisioned by Henry Kaiser in that speech five years before.

Although the Hughes-Kaiser partnership was terminated long before the only flight of the HK-1, the men remained friends. One former guest at the Kaiser home on Lake Tahoe recalled being told by "The Boss" to expect some additional guests that afternoon whom he would probably recognize. He explained that they were coming to get away from people and should be left alone. That afternoon, a seaplane landed on the lake and taxied to the dock. Out stepped Howard Hughes and his current love, Ava Gardner, one of the most alluring stars in Hollywood history.

June 15, 1944: Henry Kaiser on Film

Although based somewhat on the career of Henry Kaiser, this lobby card, signed by co-star Anne Shirley, shows a Hollywood couple bearing little resemblance to Henry and Bess Kaiser.

In 1944, Republic Pictures released a film called *Man from Frisco*. Henry Kaiser was so well known across the United States that viewers understood that this movie was actually a fictionalized account of his shipbuilding efforts in Richmond, California, and, of course, Hollywood attention only added to the Kaiser mystique.

The role of HJK was played by Michael O'Shea, an experienced actor who, although he never achieved true "star" status, did have a busy career that lasted into the 1970s. Shortly before his death, he appeared in the television series *Adam-12*. The director of *Man from Frisco* was a French import, Robert Florey, whose influence on film was so great that in 1970 the French government awarded him the Legion of Honor for his contributions to the art of the motion picture. Florey's lavish geometric dance production numbers in some of his films, including the Marx Brothers' *The Cocoanuts* (1929), inspired Busby Berkeley. Unfortunately, there was no place for a production number in *Man from Frisco*. Gene Lockhart, Dan Duryea, and Anne Shirley played the other leading roles in this movie.

One film history book summarizes the plot of the film: "A dynamic construction engineer revolutionizes shipbuilding and manages some romance on the side." Leonard Maltin, nationally syndicated movie critic and author, wrote in his *Movie and Video Guide*: "O'Shea is a pushy shipbuilding genius who meets resistance from residents of small town where he wants to build a new plant. Fairly entertaining action hokum with a little too much romance. **1/2"

After a fifteen-year search, a copy of the film was obtained by the Richmond Museum of History. Screenings have taken place at Rosie the Riveter National Park as well as on board the *Red Oak Victory*.

Gathered in the Oval Office around a model of the new Kaiser aircraft carrier are (left to right) President Roosevelt; Rear Admiral Howard Vickery, Vice Chairman of the U.S. Maritime Commission; Artemus Gates, Assistant Secretary of the Navy in charge of Naval Aviation; and Vice Admiral Emory Land, Chairman of the U.S. Maritime Commission.

Mr. Kaiser Goes to Washington*

It has been many years since one o'clock on April 12, 1945, but an entire generation can tell you where they were and what they were doing that afternoon. President Franklin Roosevelt, worn down by the strain of twelve years of leading the country, first through the Depression and then, as commander in chief, through the worst of World War II, was still exhausted from the successful but strenuous presidential campaign five months before. He was vacationing at his Warm Springs, Georgia home when he suffered a massive and fatal cerebral hemorrhage. People around the word went into mourning. The leader of the Allied nations against the Axis was dead. It was a turning point in the history of Western civilization. There would be the period before Franklin Roosevelt and the period after him.

Far less known is that almost exactly a year before, Roosevelt had expressed a preference that, if it had been carried out, would have changed the way Henry Kaiser is remembered today—and a lot of other things, too.

When Henry Met Franklin

Henry Kaiser first met Franklin Roosevelt in 1933, only two months after FDR's inauguration. Kaiser carried to the White House a letter of introduction from A.P.

---

*Much of the material for this column was drawn from the Suckley diaries as published in *Closest Companion* (edited by Geoffrey Ward, published by Houghton Mifflin, 1995) and from the archives of the FDR Presidential Library.

Giannini, president of the Bank of America. For most of the previous decade, Giannini and the Bank of America had supplied much of the capital Kaiser had needed to invest in his growing companies. It was a short but effective letter, describing HJK to a new president already keenly interested in the success of federally-sponsored public-works projects.

>Mr. President:
>
>I wish to introduce to you Mr. Henry J. Kaiser, President of Bridge Builders, Inc., one of the low bidders on the Oakland-San Francisco Bay Bridge. He is also the Executive Chairman of the Executive Committee of the Six Companies, who hold the contract on Boulder Dam.
>
>Mr. Kaiser is in Washington on matters pertaining to the Bay Bridge and while there would like to consult with you. He is a man of outstanding ability, very highly thought of in this community and has been a friend and customer since the first day he came to California.
>
>Any courtesies extended to him I shall greatly appreciate.
>
>Respectfully,
>
>A.P. Giannini

Over the years, Kaiser and FDR developed a personal relationship. Roosevelt especially appreciated Kaiser's eagerness to take on big established companies and to drive down prices through competition. Such action had helped make the New Deal work. During World War II, Kaiser had become a symbol of America's "can-do" spirit.

During the war Kaiser and his sons visited the White House a number of times on defense business, and Roosevelt and his family visited Kaiser shipyards on more than one occasion, even launching two ships. It had been FDR himself who had overruled top Navy brass after they had unanimously turned down Kaiser's plan for supplying an armada of small aircraft carriers to the battle fleets. Roosevelt, a former Secretary of the Navy, had seen the possibilities when his admirals could not. He and Kaiser had been proven right. The fifty Kaiser-built carriers had served the Navy well.

In the 1940 election, before America had entered the war, Roosevelt was running for an unprecedented third term as president. He had surprised political observers by selecting his popular Secretary of Agriculture, Henry Wallace, to replace John "Cactus Jack" Garner as "Veep."* This was a major change in the history of that office. Until then, presidents relied on their party to help in the selection. And no president had made his personal preference for vice-president so clear, but Roosevelt had good reason for breaking with tradition.

The responsibilities of the office and the increasing possibility of war meant the presidency was becoming increasingly complex. FDR wanted help, and Wallace already knew his way around Capitol Hill. Roosevelt's idea was to turn the vice-presidency into an "additional set of eyes and ears." He believed Wallace had the necessary experience to be able both to handle administrative problems and to promote Roosevelt's policies. He was dynamic as well as popular—ideal for the new role—but FDR had become disappointed in Wallace's performance. As the election of 1944 approached, it was clear that Wallace's outspoken liberal positions had turned him into a political liability. It is at this point that Henry J. Kaiser enters the presidential story.

---

* "Cactus Jack," known for his unpretentious manner and his ability to coin biting one-liners, was probably not too disappointed over this turn of events. He had been frustrated by FDR's failure to include him in important policy discussions. In a statement bowdlerized for publication in newspapers, he was quoted as saying that "the vice-presidency is not worth a bucket of warm spit."

Henry Kaiser and FDR's Cousin

For more than a half-century, until her death in 1991, Margaret "Daisy" Suckley kept a secret from the world. A distant cousin of FDR, she had been a constant companion, a good family friend to Franklin and Eleanor, and she was Roosevelt's most trusted confidante. He shared with her feelings and opinions that he could or would not share with anyone else, and no one seems to have been aware of how close the two had been. Most had regarded her as a quiet maiden lady, a pleasant, nonstressful companion for the president. She had always denied that she had kept any record of her years with the Roosevelts, so the posthumous discovery of a battered, black, diary-filled suitcase under her bed at her Hudson River estate came as a surprise to presidential scholars and historians. It took several years for the diaries to reach the public, but they were worth the wait. The volumes were filled with insights and perspectives on the man she referred to as "the P." What he said privately about world leaders, the waging of the war, cabinet members, leading politicians, and many others were carefully reported, often in Roosevelt's own words. There were a number of surprises relating to Henry Kaiser, in particular one "might-have-been" that could have changed history.

The President and his party, including Suckley, had visited Kaiser's Portland shipyards for the launching of the *SS Joseph Teal*, a ship Kaiser construction crews had launched in what was then a world-record-setting ten days. Touring the shipyard, FDR had been impressed with Kaiser's achievements, especially the innovative preassembly of huge portions of ships, which were then brought to the shipways in massive sections. Daisy Suckley wrote in her diary:

"The P. likes Mr. K. & his son Edgar who was there with him, said Mr. K is a 'dynamo.'"

'He's more like them than I am.'

FDR's favorable impressions of Kaiser on the Oregon trip, strengthened by their personal contact during Kaiser's visits to the White House, as well as a steady stream of reports he received about Kaiser's wartime productivity, mixed with HJK's growing popularity, were undoubtedly what led to a fascinating conversation between FDR and Daisy Suckley as the 1944 presidential election was approaching. The exchange was recorded by Suckley in her diary entry for May 22, 1944. Daisy and the president had been alone in a kitchen at Hyde Park. He was toasting her some of his favorite bread that Eleanor ordered for them when Suckley asked if he had decided yet on a vice-presidential candidate to replace Henry Wallace. He stunned her with his answer.

"I haven't even decided if I will run myself."

"What is going to decide you? For you are practically nominated already."

"What will decide me will be the way I feel in a couple of months. If I know I am not going to be able to carry on for another four years, it wouldn't be fair to the American people to run for another term."

"But who else is there?"

Then he shared with her the name of the one man whom he felt, if he, Roosevelt, was unable to carry on as president, could run, and win, in his place.

"I have a candidate—but don't breathe it to a soul— there is a man, not a politician, who, I think, I could persuade the country to elect. There would be such a gasp when his name was suggested, that I believe he would have a good chance if he were 'sold" to the country in the right way."

Daisy Suckley continued her diary entry:

"I did gasp a little when he mentioned the name of Henry J. Kaiser. As the P. says, it was a sudden thought on his part but the more he thinks about it, the more he sees in it. Henry J. Kaiser has proved himself a genius in production. The P. thinks he can learn where he is ignorant & without experience, such as politics, dealing with Congress, International affairs, etc."

When she asked the president how he thought Henry Kaiser would get along on the world stage with figures such as Winston Churchill, Stalin, Chiang Kai-shek, and Charles De Gaulle, she recorded Roosevelt's simple answer:

"He's more like them than I am."

Henry J. Kaiser with President Franklin D. Roosevelt during a visit to the Portland Shipyards for the launching of the SS Joseph Teal.

For many reasons, Roosevelt never publicly advanced his idea of Henry Kaiser for president or his later interest in him as a running mate. If it weren't for this entry in Daisy Suckley's diary, we wouldn't know of it at all. However, the possibility of "President Kaiser" remains an intriguing "what if." It also puts into perspective the relationship between "Hurry Up Henry" and one of the most influential leaders in American history; one more indication of Henry Kaiser's stature as a public figure as World War II came to a close.

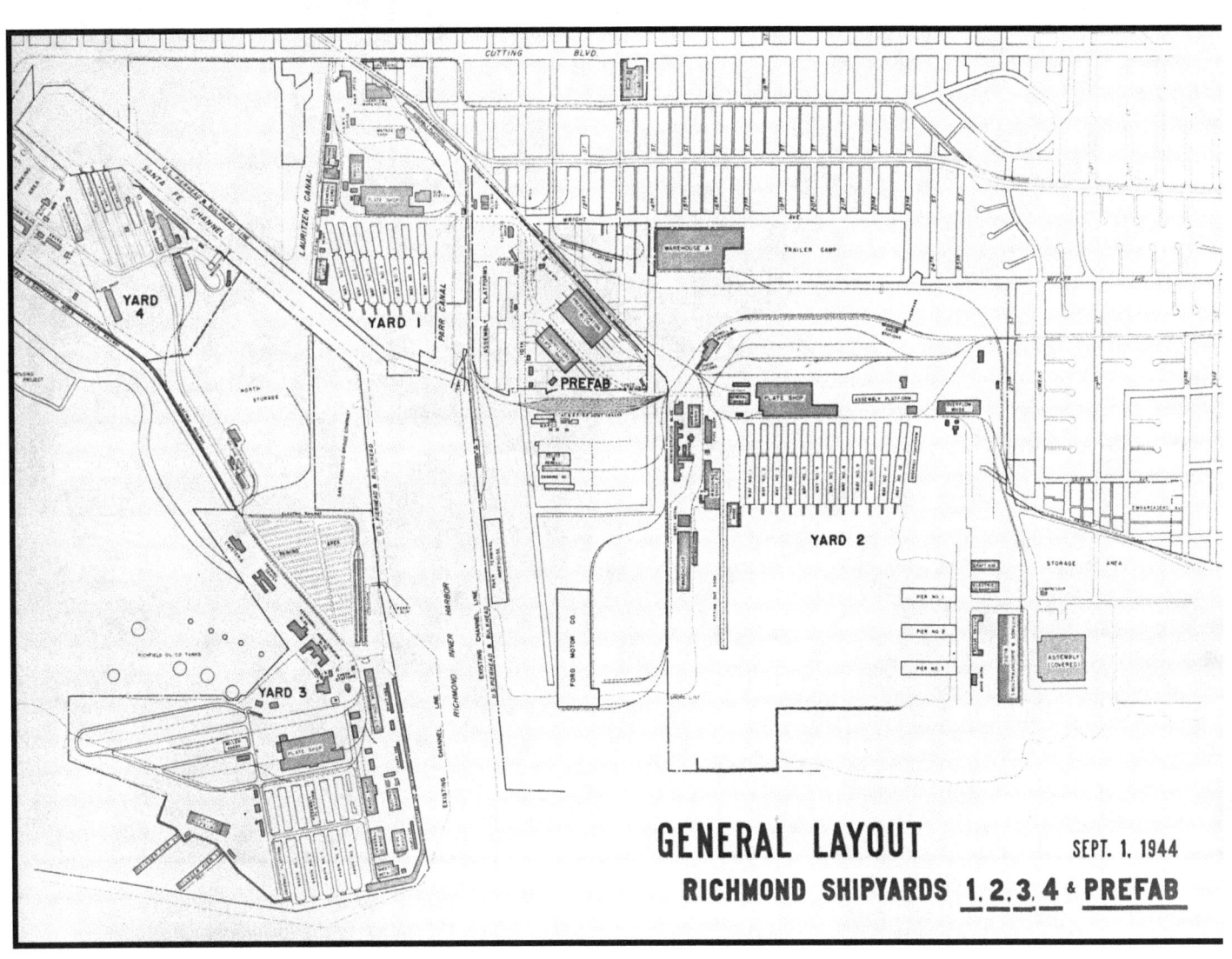

Part Two: Richmond Shipyards

Henry Kaiser with visitors from the USSR: Vyacheslav Molotov, Chairman of the Soviet Ministry of Foreign Affairs and Andrei Gromyko, Soviet Ambassador to the United States. The success of the Richmond yards made them a popular stop for visiting VIPs from the United States and abroad.

Previous Pages-
Image on left: Whirley cranes looking toward Yard No. 2 shipways.
Image on right: Shipyards No. 1 and No. 2 built Liberty ships and Victory ships. Yard No. 3 built troop transports. Yard No. 4 produced LSTs (Landing Ship, Tank), frigates, and "pint-size" Liberties, mostly with parts prefabricated all over the country and assembled in Richmond.

Hitler Knew About Richmond

In the fall, 1940, Richmond, California, was not a city name familiar in the capitals of Europe and Asia. Within three years that had changed dramatically. By then, Hitler knew about Richmond. So did Hideki Tojo, the Japanese imperial warlord. And so did Winston Churchill, Charles deGaulle, Joseph Stalin, and, of course, Franklin Roosevelt. In fact, all the leaders of the great powers involved in World War II knew about Richmond. In a war that would be defined and decided by a nation's ability to carry combat to enemy shores, Richmond's shipbuilding prowess became a shining example to the Allies and a grim warning to their Axis adversaries. Ships from the four Kaiser shipyards in Richmond and from the more than twenty-five other yards along San Francisco Bay were delivering massive amounts of troops, supplies, and weapons to the world's battlefields. They were making possible what would become a complete and total Allied victory. Not long before, people had measured the time needed to build a ship in years. Now, every day, one brand-new ship was sailing through the Golden Gate to take her place in the war fleets of the world. In addition to the materiel of modern warfare, each carried the justifiable pride of her builders.

The people of Richmond, in particular, had every reason to be proud of their accomplishments. During the war years, Richmond yards alone produced 747 ships. Richmond-built ships participated in every major sea campaign of the war, in every ocean. Richmond shipyards were producing more ships, and they were doing it faster and better, than had ever been done at anytime in the history of the world.

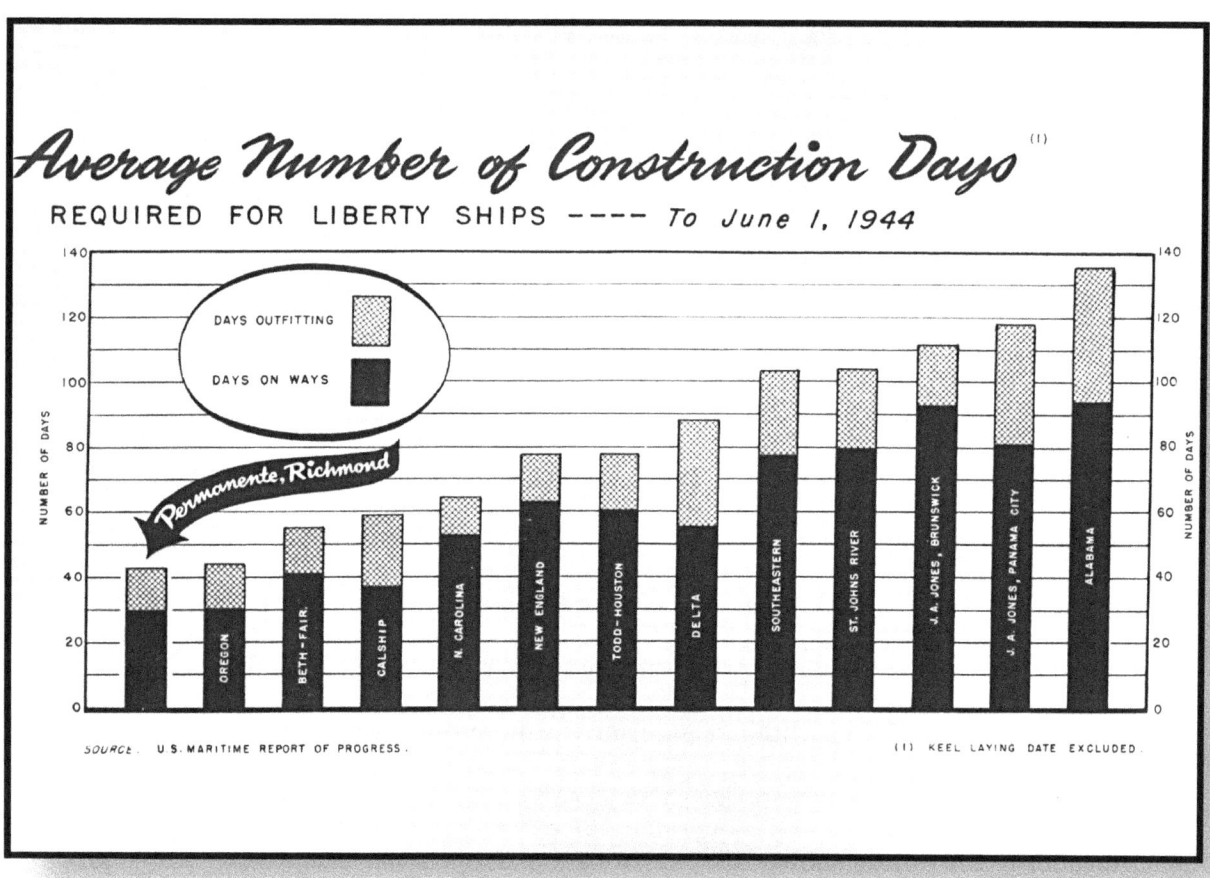

The only shipyards that came close to matching Richmond (far left column) in speed of building Liberty ships were the Kaiser yards in Oregon. A postwar investigation showed that these ships, from Richmond and Portland, ranked with the best built by any shipyard.

When the Richmond Yard No. 2 reduced the time needed to build a ship to four days, the feat became a symbol of American determination, of Yankee ingenuity, and of the fact that when a free nation becomes aroused and begins to fight for its liberty, there's no limit to what its people can accomplish.

Explosive Growth, Liberty Ships, *and the Poet from Oakland*

July 14, 1942 was the day of the launching of the *SS Edward Rowland Sill*. Only a year and a half had elapsed since Henry Kaiser had won a contract to build thirty ships and just seven months since Japan's attack on Pearl Harbor had awakened the America that Admiral Yamamoto (architect of the assault) called "a sleeping giant." American industry was moving into high gear, and Richmond, California, was well along in its transformation from a small, quiet industrial city with a small-town feel into one of the most vital industrial centers of the home front.

Kaiser's first shipyard did not produce Liberty ships—as yet there was no such thing as a Liberty ship. His contract was to build thirty freighters for the British government. It didn't bother him that he had neither experience building ships nor even a shipyard. Later he would say rather proudly that when he and "his boys" had gone into shipbuilding, he knew so little about ships that he talked about the "front end" and "back end" of vessels. Even so, he had convinced the British, desperate for new ships, to underwrite the costs of building a shipyard and to give him the technical help he needed to get underway. In return, he would see that they got their ships on or ahead of schedule. The challenge seemed to energize him.

Kaiser also saw a potential for shipbuilding that went far beyond this single contract. War for the United States was beginning to appear inevitable. In January

1941, President Roosevelt had initiated the Liberty ship program, the biggest shipbuilding project in history. HJK was determined to carve out a chunk of it for his company. With American entry into the war, he could see that fighting would take place on two oceans, but most U.S. shipyards were on the East Coast. A West Coast shipbuilder would have major advantages. Kaiser knew he could keep a Richmond yard busy after he had completed the contract for the thirty freighters, but he would need to have steel, which was already in short supply. With the whole nation arming, building tanks, jeeps, artillery, and aircraft, he was sure the shortage would only get worse. He lobbied the federal government for permission to build a steel plant in Southern California where he would be able to manufacture his own steel plate. In March 1942, on land that had hosted pig farms, he began construction. Just nine months later, the brand new plant was producing pig iron.

He would also need more shipbuilding facilities. As soon as the plan for the construction of Liberty ships was announced, HJK sent his older son, Edgar, to Portland-Vancouver to buy land along the Columbia River. Edgar purchased eighty-seven acres on the Columbia River and began constructing what would become Oregonship in Portland, the first of three Kaiser Northwest shipyards. (The other two were Swan Island and Vancouver.) Simultaneously, Kaiser began constructing a second shipyard in Richmond to build the new Liberty ships.

This period was an amazing time in this now sixty-year-old man's life. As huge an undertaking as his shipbuilding program was becoming, it certainly hadn't overtaxed his energies. He kept looking for additional business opportunities.

Kaiser asked for and received federal clearance to build a magnesium plant on the San Francisco Peninsula near Cupertino at Permanente, California where he was already producing cement. Magnesium, a lightweight metal, was in great demand by the U.S. military for planes and munitions. Kaiser discovered that he could integrate heat processes used in magnesium production with those needed in cement manufacture. He could produce magnesium cheaper and more efficiently than was currently possible.

Even with all this activity, Kaiser still possessed excess organizational energy! In January 1942 Kaiser signed a contract to build Yard No. 3. This new shipyard was designed to be different from the first two: rather than another temporary yard built for the wartime emergency, this one was to function as an industrial hub. The shipways were to be dry docks where, after the war, ships could be repaired as well as built. Kaiser was already planning for the postwar period.

While Yard One completed the contract for the British freighters, Yard Two began constructing American Liberty ships. Because Kaiser had had to build his shipyards from scratch and because he was still building the British freighters, Kaiser was not the first to launch a Liberty ship. In September 1941, on Liberty Fleet Day, in a dawn-to-dusk display of American industrial might, fourteen Liberty ships had been launched in shipyards across the country. Kaiser's first Liberty launch took place on December 31, 1941. But even with his later start, Kaiser's innovations would revolutionize ship production with techniques still employed in modern shipyards.

One of Kaiser's first Liberty ships was the *Edward Rowland Sill*. Since Kaiser had some authority to name the ships in this class from a list of prominent Americans, I thought it would be interesting to find out just who Edward Sill was. The first reference I found to him came in a book of quotations: "Be satisfied with nothing but your best." That sentiment certainly matched Henry Kaiser's thinking. E.R. Sill (1841-1887) was a nationally-known poet from Oakland, Henry Kaiser's adopted home town. He was a favorite of poet Robert Frost as well as HJK. Sill had been a teacher in Oakland and then superintendent of schools before moving to Palo Alto to become a professor at Stanford. I could imagine Kaiser savoring Sill's poem about the nobleness of doing the best you can with what you have to work with.

Opportunity

This I beheld, or dreamed it in a dream:

There spread a cloud of dust along a plain;

And underneath the cloud, or in it, raged

A furious battle, and men yelled, and swords

Shocked upon swords and shields. A prince's banner

Wavered, then staggered backward, hemmed by foes.

A craven hung along the battle's edge,

And thought, "Had I a sword of keener steel—

That blue blade that the king's son bears—but this

Blunt thing—!" He snapped and flung it from his hand,

And lowering crept away and left the field.

Then came the king's son, wounded sore bestead,

And weaponless, and saw the broken sword,

Hilt-buried in the dry and trodden sand,

And ran and snatched it, and with battle shout

Lifted afresh he hewed his enemy down,

And saved a great cause that heroic day.

As Henry Kaiser was entering his seventh decade and still picking up speed, and even as he was accomplishing more and more in a lifetime already filled with notable achievements, he must have had a sense of his own mortality. It is easy to think of him reflecting on this verse by the man for whom he named a Liberty ship.

Life

Forenoon and afternoon and night,—
And day is gone,—
So short a span of time there is
'Twixt dawn and evensong.
Youth,—Middle life,—Old age,—
And life is past,—
So live each day that God shall say,
"Well done!" at last.

The Oakland poet, Edward R. Sill, one of Henry Kaiser's favorites.

The *SS Edward Rowland Sill* took part in the Normandy D-day invasion in 1944. In 1967, she returned to San Francisco Bay, where she was scrapped.

Aiming to Deliver

The Armed Guard, whose motto was "We Aim to Deliver," was formed by the Navy in October 1941 to provide gun crews to defend U.S. merchant ships. After three weeks of training, the first gun crews were ready to sail in November 1941, when Congress repealed the Neutrality Act.

The emblem for the U.S. Navy Armed Guards serving aboard the merchant ships was the eagle hovering protectively over the oceans with a German submarine and a Japanese fighter clasped in its talons.

By war's end, more than 144,900 men had served on over 6,000 American and Allied ships and nearly 2,000 had given their lives for their ships and for their country.

The Gallant Ship
SS Stephen Hopkins

One of the most unusual and heroic sea battles of World War II took place on a Sunday morning off the coast of South Africa on September 27, 1942, exactly one year after "Liberty Fleet Day." On that day in 1941, in a massive display of American production power, fourteen Liberty ships had been launched at shipyards around the United States to be a part of the "bridge of ships" carrying war supplies to Allied armies around the globe. That anniversary morning, *SS Stephen Hopkins*, built in Richmond Yard No. 2, came out of the fog of a South Atlantic rain squall. The *Hopkins* was on her maiden voyage and, having dropped off part of her cargo in New Zealand, was en route from South Africa to Paramaribo in Dutch Guiana (today's Surinam) to pick up a load of bauxite, aluminum ore. Two miles ahead, the lookouts spotted what turned out to be the German commerce raider *Stier*, taking advantage of the poor visibility while taking on supplies from her armed escort, the *Tannenfels*.

The German ship was cruising these waters looking for Allied freighters. She had been designed to seek out and destroy merchant ships like the *Hopkins*, and she was well equipped for the task. Faster than the *Hopkins*, she was armed with six 5.9-inch guns, two 37-MM guns, four 20-MM guns, and two torpedo tubes. She had another major advantage—modern gun-directors and fire-control. This was a dangerous enemy. A similarly armed raider had sunk a battle-hardened cruiser with all hands in a point-blank gun duel just a few months earlier.

Stier carried a crew of 324, which, now experienced in high seas warfare, had recently sunk one tanker and two freighters similar to the *Hopkins*. When the Germans spotted the lightly-armed American freighter coming towards them, they prepared for another victory.

Fregattenkapitän Horst Gerlach ordered the *Hopkins* to heave-to, but Captain Paul Buck refused and, ignoring a warning shot, turned his ship around to present a smaller target to the German gunners who began firing in earnest at the fleeing Liberty ship.

The *Hopkins* was seriously outmanned and outgunned. Her largest weapon was a single World War I-era four-inch naval cannon mounted on the stern, The gun captain, Ensign Kenneth Willett put the gun into action, but almost immediately he was gravely wounded as a piece of shrapnel slashed into his belly. However, the dying man, using one hand to hold in his insides, somehow managed to continue directing the gun crew's fire with great effect.

One of the first salvos from the *Stier* struck the upper works of the *Hopkins*, severely wounding Chief Mate Richard Moczkowski. Moczkowski had grown up in Richmond, not far from where his ship had been built. Although gravely wounded, he propped himself up on the bridge, staying at his post to assist Captain Buck in steering the ship. Together the two managed to keep the stern pointed toward the pursuing enemy reducing the chance of being hit while making it easier for the gun crew to bring their own gun to bear on the enemy.

Shell after shell from the *Hopkins*' old four-inch gun was striking the *Stier* with astonishing accuracy. The Germans now directed their fire at the gun, hoping to silence it. Several times they nearly succeeded, killing or wounding the sailors firing it. However, each time, new volunteers rushed to replace their fallen mates and kept the cannon firing back. The *Tannenfels* joined the fray. She carried an even larger gun, a six-inch cannon, but her crew was unable to hit the *Hopkins*.

Both ships were taking a terrible beating. Within half an hour they were close enough to each other for small arms fire. German and American machine guns raked enemy decks. Both vessels were so damaged that each now was dead in the water. The German and the American ships were on fire, with water pouring uncontrollably into their hulls where enemy shells had blown holes near the waterline.

The *Stier* and the *Hopkins* were sinking.

When Captain Buck gave the order to abandon ship, eighteen-year-old Merchant Marine Cadet Edwin O'Hara clambered up from his battle station in the engine room and saw his severely-wounded friend Ken Willett, lying on the gun platform. O'Hara helped him down to the deck and made him as comfortable as he could. He then returned to the gun where he had seen five shells still in the shot locker. Although damaged, the cannon was still operable. Single-handedly O'Hara, under withering automatic weapons fire, loaded, aimed, and fired the big gun five times. Each one of his shots struck the enemy. He even hit the pursuing *Tannenfels*, which, although further away, had taken up the chase.

It was now obvious that nothing could save the *Hopkins*. She was sinking. *Fregattenkapitän* Gerlach ordered a cease-fire so that his men could concentrate on saving his own badly-damaged ship, and, not long after that, the *Hopkins*, burning and battered, slipped under the waves taking most of her crew with her. Fifteen crewmembers, including five of the Armed Guard, did survive the fierce sea battle and made it to land. They had managed to launch a lifeboat and sailed across the South Atlantic for thirty-one days until they reached the coast of Brazil.

While the *Hopkins* had been lost, her crew had done something that had been thought impossible: the merchant ship had sunk a German navy warship that had outgunned and outmanned her. At a time when there was little good war news, the bravery and dedication of the crew of the *Hopkins* brought hope to Americans.

The title "Gallant Ship" is a high honor. It may be awarded "to any United States ship or to any foreign ship (merchant, Coast Guard, Navy, or other) participating in outstanding or gallant action," but the standards are very high. Of the thousands of vessels that took part in World War II, only nine have been considered deserving of this award. The *SS Hopkins* is a Gallant Ship.

For their bravery and for their achievement, the crew of the *Hopkins* received a number of medals, many of them posthumously. Three Liberty Ships were christened in the names of crewmembers: the *SS Paul Buck*, *SS Edwin Joseph O'Hara*, and *SS Richard Moczkowski*; a destroyer escort, the *USS Kenneth M. Willett* (DE-354).

The *SS Stephen Hopkins* itself received another special honor when in May, 1944, a newly-christened *SS Stephen Hopkins II*, slid down a shipway at Kaiser's Yard No. 2 in Richmond to carry on the fight.

On the occasion of the launch of the SS Richard Moczkowski, *August 22, 1943, Richmond Shipyard No. 2. At the side of Henry Kaiser is Ernest K. Lindley, head of Newsweek's Washington, D.C. bureau and writer of his own column, "Washington Tides." The ship was named in memory of the chief mate of the* SS Stephen Hopkins, *the merchant ship that sunk a German Navy warship in 1942. Ships were named after Moczkowski and three others of his crew for their bravery.*

SS Robert E. Peary:
"The Wonder Ship"

In 1942, the Kaiser shipyard in Richmond, California astonished the world by building a ship in 4 days, 15 hours and 29 minutes, setting a record that probably will never be beaten. At precisely 3:26 on the afternoon of November 12, 1942, the Liberty ship *SS Robert E. Peary*, the famous Hull No. 440, slid down a shipway at Kaiser Shipyard No. 2 in Richmond, California, into San Francisco Bay. Enthusiastic cheers of the thousands of spectators were nearly drowned out by band music and blasts from every shipyard horn and whistle. The celebration capped an extraordinary event: Kaiser shipyard workers had assembled this entire 7,176-ton ship, 441-1/2 feet from stem to stern, in just four-and-a-half days.

Only a year before, the U.S. Maritime Commission, the "client" for the Liberty ships, had estimated that on a speeded-up schedule it should take 250 days to build a ship like this. By late 1942, there were eighteen shipyards building Liberties and the average construction time for most of the yards was down to sixty days. The Kaiser "Build them by the mile, cut them off by the yard" approach to mass production had cut the average in their yards further, to a very impressive thirty-five days per ship. Furthermore, the Kaiser vessels were built well, something much appreciated by their officers and crews. The nearly 200,000 people working for Kaiser were fiercely proud of their achievements in shipbuilding.

The story of "The Wonder Ship" had begun several months before launching. In late summer 1942, Edgar Kaiser, Henry Kaiser's son and the general manager of the Kaiser shipyards in the Vancouver-Portland area, had called on the workers there to set a new speed record, far surpassing anything done before. The workers had responded with great energy and enthusiasm, resulting in the launch, on September 23, of the *S.S. Joseph Teal* in just ten days. This was a new world's record, smashing the previous one which, incidentally, had been held by the Kaiser Richmond yards. It was such a significant achievement that President Roosevelt made a secret trip across country and attended the launching. And it was his daughter, Anna Boettiger, who broke the traditional bottle of champagne across the bow.

When Edgar Kaiser's counterpart, Clay Bedford, general manager of Kaiser's Richmond yards, returned from the *Teal* launching in Portland, he was determined to reclaim for Richmond the title of the "World's Fastest Shipbuilders" and the bragging rights that went with it. He set his staff on the problem of how to organize the building of a ship to have it completed in significantly less than the ten days it had taken Edgar Kaiser's crews. Line workers were asked for their suggestions of how to speed up production. Many of the suggestions proved useful. A sense of competition, a spirit highly valued in the Kaiser organization, spurred the group on. They became determined to win back the shipbuilding title. Before long, Bedford had the elements of a plan that benefited from the experience and imagination of literally thousands of workers. Details were checked, refined, and checked again. The progress of every one of the 250,000 parts that went into a Liberty ship, 14,000,000 pounds of them, was laid out in precise order. It started to become clear that the record-breaking ship would not only set a new record, it would be a real-world laboratory for new techniques, which, if they worked, would become standard operating procedure.

During the weeks leading up to the assembly of Hull 440, huge prefabricated sections, including the bow, stern, and deck sections, began to take shape around the shipyard. The pieces reminded some of the workers of a giant jigsaw puzzle scattered through the yard.

Alyce Kramer, in *Story of the Richmond Shipyards*, describes the start of construction of "The Wonder Ship":

Two welders working on the deck of the Robert E. Peary *on the second day of assembly, November 9, 1942.*

> *Yard Two became hushed in the silent awe that precedes the critical engagement. Her people had publicly promised America a second home front in the form of the fastest shipbuilding job in history. At the stroke of twelve [midnight], Way One exploded into life. Crews of workers, like a championship football team, swarmed to their places in the line. Within 60 seconds, the keel was swinging into position. . . . The speed was unbelievable. At midnight Saturday, an empty way; at midnight Sunday, a full-grown hull met the eyes of graveyard [shift] workers as they came on shift. . . . Feverish, yet sure and methodical, was the march against time. Orders were explicit, work was controlled, muscles were strained, hearts were bursting with hope and pride ...*

The huge bow section, one of the first prefabricated pieces to be put in place, was so completely prefabricated that even the ship's name was already painted on it. The deckhouse, a 250-ton section of the ship, was totally assembled before the building of the ship began. The 26,000 feet of welding, all five miles needed to complete the deckhouse, had been done, and the deck house already contained the necessary electric appliances, floorings, plumbing, and fixtures. Crews' quarters in the deckhouse were fitted out with bunks, chests of drawers, sinks, and toilets, even mirrors. However, at 250 tons, the preassembled deckhouse was too heavy even for the brawny whirley cranes to lift, so the shipyard planners decided on an ingenious strategy. Once the deckhouse had been completely assembled, they cut it into four roughly equal parts. Shipyard cranes could lift these more manageable sixty-seventy-ton pieces aboard the ship where they were joined back together with just 600 feet of additional welding. The time saved on the ways by prefabrication was enormous.

The speed continued even after the *Peary* was launched. Just ten days after the ship slid down the ways, she had completed her sea trials, taken on a crew, and had been loaded with the equivalent of three hundred railroad cars of vital war materiel. On November 22, a ship that hadn't existed two weeks before steamed out through the Golden Gate carrying a cargo of food and war supplies to the South Pacific. It was a phenomenal achievement.

Of course there were detractors. Some said it had been nothing more than a publicity stunt. After all, the ship had been almost totally preassembled. Clay Bedford was quick to point out that that had been the whole purpose—to see how much more ship construction could be done in timesaving preassembly, thereby freeing-up valuable space on the shipways for more ship construction.

Other people claimed the ship had been thrown together for speed, without regard for the quality of construction. However, a War Shipping Administration report later silenced those critics. "In her first year of war cargo transport," the report stated, "the *Robert E. Peary* voyaged more than 42,000 miles. Master's and Engineer's Reports show that her mechanical and navigational efficiency equals that of sister ships much longer on the ways."

She was a hero, too. On her first voyage, the *Peary* saved American soldiers trapped near the beach of a Japanese-held Pacific island. While under enemy fire, the *Peary* maneuvered close to shore. The sailors rigged a line to the beach which they used to ferry food and ammunition to the troops until they were able to beat back the Japanese attack. The *Peary* also participated in the D-day invasion on the other side of the world, shuttling back and forth between England and the Allied beachhead in Normandy, often under heavy air attack.

In the pages of *Fore 'N' Aft*, the shipyard's weekly magazine, written "by and for" the shipyard workers, the Kaiser company kept the workers informed of the achievements of their ship. They never had reason to be anything but proud of "The Wonder Ship" they had built in just 111-1/2 hours.

After twenty-one years of service, the *SS Robert E. Peary* was scrapped in Baltimore, Maryland, June 1963.

Aerial view of Richmond with Yard No. 3 in foreground.
The large white building in right center of the photograph is the General Warehouse, a landmark in the Rosie the Riveter Park today. Following the longitudinal axis of the building on either side are buildings still standing. Further to the right, along the longitudinal axis of the two ships pictured, is where the Red Oak Victory *is currently berthed. The ship closest to the bottom of the photograph is where the record-breaking* SS Robert E. Peary *was launched on November 12, 1942. No marker exists to memorialize this unequal achievement.*

Unidentified worker at Shipyard No. 1 showing his height on chart behind him.

Streams of workers head for the shipyard gates and homeward at the end of their shift.

The People Who Built Her

Any fair-minded person looking at the accomplishments of the first members of the Kaiser Richmond shipyard workforce has to admit they were an amazing group of people. They were the ones who, when speed was most needed, surprised the world by launching a Liberty ship in twenty-four days; then, at another Kaiser shipyard, they launched a Liberty in just ten days, a new world's record. And then, not long after that, they launched the *Robert E. Peary* in just a little more than four-and-a-half days—a breathtaking achievement in an industry where not long before shipbuilding had been measured in years.

This group of shipyard employees, eventually numbering nearly 200,000 men and women, were an unlikely group of heavy-industry record-setters. Many of the men hired after America's entry into the war were unfit for military service due to health or age, resulting in a workforce with an unusually high proportion of health problems. Most had arrived at the shipyards without a clue about how to build ships. Among the first people hired to work in the yards were experienced construction workers and foremen from Grand Coulee Dam. Their record there had been admirable. It had been the largest public works construction project in history; bigger even than the Great Pyramid. Many experts had given reason after reason why it would be impossible to build that huge dam, but these would-be shipbuilders were some of the people who had been responsible not only for completing it but getting it done ahead of schedule and under budget.

For many of these workers, the shipyard shore was their first glimpse of the ocean. Filled with the self-confidence of having already achieved the "impossible," they shared Henry Kaiser's belief that they could apply industrial and organizational techniques honed at Boulder, Bonneville, and Grand Coulee dams to building ships. Soon they would give the "professionals" another surprise. The ex-dam workers were soon joined by ex-clerks, ex-farmhands, ex-salesmen, ex-almost everything except ex-shipbuilders. Although inexperienced (according to a 1942 estimate only one in a hundred had any shipbuilding experience), these were people who, for the most part, brought to their jobs a deep-rooted desire to do something important for the war effort.

With so few people familiar with the vocabulary of the sea, the newcomers' language took on some strange word usage as they replaced unfamiliar maritime words with their own. For instance, the hold of a ship became known in the yards as the "hole." Because "hole" was appropriately descriptive and few knew any better, soon almost everyone was using it. It even found its way into writing. Another seafaring word that almost disappeared was "caulking." This is the process by which small gaps in a ship are filled with various compounds to make the vessel watertight. It soon became known as "corking," again descriptive, if not traditional. A more mysterious word-morphing related to a ship's kitchen. Known to sailors for hundreds of years as the "galley," it was renamed in the Kaiser workers' lexicon as "the gallery," although the reason for its selection to replace an unfamiliar word is not as clear as it is for "hole" and "corking."

It isn't hard to imagine what the few old-timers who had spent decades in ship construction thought of these shipbuilding Johnnies-come-lately who couldn't even get the words right. However, when these same work crews, using methods of mass production, started turning out "ships by the mile and cutting them off by the yard," the experienced hands had to reassess their first impressions. Grudgingly or not, they had to admit that nobody had ever built ships faster, and that their quality was as good as or better than those of even the veteran shipyards building this emergency fleet.

By the time the *Robert E. Peary* was built, the shortage of shipyard workers had become acute. Kaiser sent recruiters throughout the Dust Bowl and to the states where Depression-level unemployment still held sway. With the promise of shipyard jobs, men signed up by the hundreds. They were put on Kaiser Specials, trains bound for the Richmond and Columbia River shipyards. With the need for construction workers growing so fast, one man remembered that on the afternoon he had applied for work at the Kaiser hiring office, there had been another man waiting, hoping to find a job. He had partially recovered from a stroke. His left side was still severely weakened, but the hiring officials were busy looking for a job for him where he could put his good right side to work!

However, as much as the shipyards needed workers, Kaiser had only been able to hire men to work in the yards. That had begun to change in July 1942 when a group of women demonstrated outside the San Francisco headquarters of the International Brotherhood of Boilermakers, Iron Shipbuilders and Helpers of America. This was the most powerful of the shipyard unions; it would not accept women as members, and Kaiser was unable to hire anyone who did not have a union card. Before the war, before anyone knew how big the shipyards would grow, Kaiser and other shipbuilders had signed an agreement with the union, which, among other things, offered them a "closed" shop in return for a no-strike pledge. This meant that when women wanted to come into the shipyards as construction workers, they found that they were in effect frozen out.

The demonstration in July helped to highlight both the unfairness of the practice and how it interfered with the war effort. The Boilermakers, now under pressure, reconsidered. After a few weeks the shipyard magazine, *Fore 'N' Aft*, announced the hiring of the first ten female welders. Later, when it was announced that an attempt to break the world's record for speed in shipbuilding would be made with the construction of the *Robert E. Peary*, thirteen

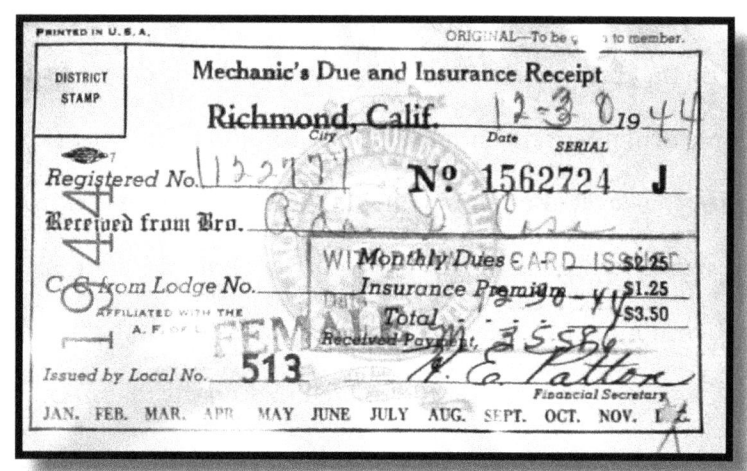
Union dues receipt bearing the "Female" stamp.

women welders volunteered. They even threatened to quit if they weren't chosen for the work crew. Women soon proved their value on the job, and within two years, women made up more than a quarter of the shipyard labor force.

Some of the "inexperienced" shipbuilders brought special skills to their new jobs. Riggers had to scamper skillfully across the tall stagings that towered over each hull under construction, hooking and unhooking heavy craneloads of steel and other supplies being moved about the shipway. They often had to leap from two-by-fours onto mast poles or walk across two inch rails over a "hole" fifty feet deep. Experienced riggers did this with a much-admired agility and a grace that often provided entertainment to the workers below. At Richmond, there was one crew of riggers that was particularly good at this sort of work. It was made up primarily of ex-ballet dancers. For them, rigging was an extension of an art they had practiced for years.

One of the flangers had a very appropriate background that prepared him well for his shipbuilding assignment. He was an ex-wrestler. As a flanger, his job now was to beat, pull, twist, and push stubborn steel bulkheads (a ship's interior walls) into their correct position. He was one of the best.

By the time the keel of the record-breaking *Robert E. Peary* was laid down, the Kaiser shipyards had a year-and-a-half of experience. Everyone had learned a lot. Management took advantage of this by asking for suggestions from the people on the front lines of production. They came in literally by the hundreds and the thousands. Each was evaluated. Some suggestions saved a few minutes or a few dollars; some saved badly-needed material; and a few saved hundreds of worker-hours per ship or were especially valuable because they reduced the chances of on-the-job injury.

The Kaiser company always made a point of showing its appreciation for ideas that were adopted. The best ones were featured, along with their originators, in the shipyard magazines, improving morale while encouraging more workers to step forward with their ideas.

The launching of the *Peary* caught America's attention and admiration. It was headline news across the nation. While the Kaiser shipyards were proud of their achievement, the whole country looked to what the Kaiser workforce had done as a symbol of what can be accomplished by combining the organizational ability of American industry with the energy, enthusiasm, and Yankee ingenuity of the workers to produce the tools of war that would defeat the Axis powers.

A predominantly African-American work crew poses for the camera.

In some communities, employers dislike to employ women. In others, they are reluctant to hire Negroes. In still others, older men are not wanted. We can no longer afford to indulge such prejudices or practices.

—President Franklin D. Roosevelt, 1942

African-American Liberty Ships
and the Kaiser Shipyards

Crippled by more than a decade of the Great Depression, the United States began the 1940s by mobilizing at top speed to carry on an overseas war. Few people were aware of how powerful a driving force for change that war would be within America. One way was through employment. The need for workers to fill vital defense-related jobs opened new opportunities to millions of Americans.

As the 1940s began, the country was sliding inexorably towards World War II. Three out of four African Americans still lived in the South. They held the unenviable distinction of being the poorest people in America's poorest region. In the country as a whole, statistically, African Americans were more likely than their white countrymen to work as unskilled laborers, and when they did, they earned 60 percent less than what whites earned doing the same job. Adjusting today's standards to the economy of sixty-plus years ago, nearly nine out of ten African Americans could be considered to have been living below the federal poverty level. As the war approached, though, 2.5 million African-American men lined up to register for the draft, and thousands of black women volunteered for military duty. On the home front, black Americans supported the war effort by taking jobs in war industries—when they could get them. Tens of thousands left their homes in the South for the Western states or wherever there was promise of employment.

Despite the labor shortage, some companies were reluctant to hire African Americans, but Kaiser was not one of them. Kaiser sent recruiting teams into the Dust

Bowl states and into the Deep South looking for workers. As one shipyard executive said, "We do not ask what their color is."

While thousands of African Americans were working in the Kaiser shipyards along the Columbia River and the San Francisco Bay, thousands more were sailing those ships. Ten percent of the Merchant Marine Service—24,000 men—were African Americans, and they were serving on integrated ships. Unlike the Army and Navy, which were still segregated, merchant mariners served in all capacities, from the lower positions such as messman and engine wiper, up into all levels of all departments, including engineering, as deck officers, and even as captains. Although discrimination existed, it was not as evident in the Merchant Marines as it was in the armed services.

Not all white workers were comfortable with the changes going on around them. Al Smith, an African-American from Texas working for Kaiser in Richmond, recalled that in the shipyard at the time, "A lot of those southerners, those white, die-hard southerners, that didn't like blacks period, got here, too. And those Southerners thought, 'Well, we're going to do exactly what we've been doing down in the south,' but it didn't work. It didn't work, you know, because it was different here."

One reason "it was different here" was that there was a growing understanding in Washington and among more progressive employers, such as Henry Kaiser, that the contributions of African Americans had become an important part of the war effort. Such realizations led to a government decision to produce a series of Liberty ships named after prominent black Americans. Seventeen such ships were authorized. Several more were named for historically black colleges and universities. Contracts for these ships seem to have been carefully spread over the country in order to maximize their impact. The African-Americans honored were:

Robert S. Abbott

George Washington Carver

Frederick Douglass

John Hope

George A. Lawson

John H. Murphy

Harriett Tubman

James K. Walker

Robert J. Banks

William Cox

Paul Laurence Dunbar

James Weldon Johnson

John Merrick

Edward A. Savoy

Robert L. Vann

Booker T. Washington

Bert Williams

Of the seventeen ships, contracts to build three went to Kaiser yards, specifically Yards No. 1 and No. 2 in Richmond. The first was the *SS George Washington Carver*, launched May 7, 1943 (just months after the scientist's death). Although it is well-known that Dr. Carver invented a hundred uses for peanuts and hundreds more for soybeans, pecans, and sweet potatoes, it is less appreciated what a difference this made in the lives of many people, black and white. New uses made these crops more valuable for the small farmers who produced them, saving thousands of family farms. Carver also developed agricultural techniques that rescued farmland exhausted from growing cotton, allowing it to remain productive. Even though his discoveries could have earned him a fortune, Carver patented very few of them. Most he gave away, so as many people as possible could benefit from them.

The launching of the *SS George Washington Carver* was a festive event. Al Smith, raised on a sharecropper farm in rural east Texas and working at Kaiser Yard No. 1, was still fairly new in Richmond at the time. He remembers how impressed he was with the activities surrounding the launching.

Launch of the SS George Washington Carver, *the second in a series of African-American-named ships, May 7, 1943. Lena Horne, actress, singer, and dancer brought added glamour to the launching that held much meaning for the African-American community.*

I remember the time that they launched the George Washington Carver ship. [laughs] I had never seen such fantastic looking black people in all of my life. The ladies with the heels and I think they even had fur stoles on. And I just could've stared with wonder— and I just went, "That is something else." I loved the way they presented themselves. The lady hit the ship and the champagne flew all over and the ship went down into the water.

The second of the three ships, *SS John Hope*, was launched January 30, 1944, also at Richmond Yard No. 1. John Hope (1868-1936) had spent his life in the struggle for

100   *"Build 'Em by the Mile, Cut 'Em off by the Yard"*

racial equality through the education of African American youth. He also participated in the founding of the NAACP.

The *SS Robert S. Abbott*, launched at Kaiser Yard No. 2 on April 13, 1944, was named after the publisher of the *Chicago Defender*, one of the longest-running national newspapers dedicated to informing African Americans. Abbott (1869-1940) is considered to have been one of the outstanding spokesmen for black Americans of his time.

Executive Order 8802

On June 25, 1941, more than five months before Pearl Harbor, President Roosevelt signed Executive Order 8802, the Fair Employment Act, to regulate hiring in the defense industries. The order required all federal agencies and departments involved with defense production to ensure that vocational and training programs were administered without discrimination as to "race, creed, color, or national origin." From then on, all defense contracts were to include provisions barring private contractors from discriminating as well. Although it was not a law and had no real enforcement provision, it was the first federal action, to promote equal opportunity and prohibit employment discrimination.

The president issued his executive order as a response to pressure from civil rights activists Bayard Rustin, A. Philip Randolph, and A. J. Muste, who wanted to ensure that African Americans benefited from the thousands of new jobs that were being created by federal defense contracts. The activists had been planning a march on Washington, D.C. to protest racial discrimination. After President Roosevelt issued Executive Order 8802, the march was called off.

The October 1, 1943 issue of the Richmond shipyard magazine, Fore 'N' Aft, featured the Liberty ships being built for America's Chinese allies.

The Chinese Liberty Ships

Leola Chow began working in the Kaiser shipyards in Richmond early in World War II. For a year she worked in Yard No. 3 as an estimator, keeping track of all electrical materials that went into each ship. She joined the Health Plan at that time. Although she enjoyed the shipyard work, she had to leave the job when time drew near for her daughter to be born.

When Mrs. Chow was ready to go back to work, she was only interested in working the swing shift, working nights so that she could spend her days with her infant daughter. But that meant she couldn't go back to her old job at Yard Three. Working swing shift there would have meant traveling back and forth to work on public transportation, by herself, at night, a prospect she found very unpleasant. Luckily, the Richmond Field Hospital was much closer to her home, and when she applied for a job there, she was hired as a receptionist. This surprised her a little because she had no experience in that sort of work. Before long, though, she found out why she had been hired. Because she was fluent in both English and Chinese, the hospital had wanted her on staff in order to have someone available to act as translator on the swing shift. Translators were important because there were a great many Chinese-American workers in the shipyards. Hundreds, if not more, spoke no English at all. When they needed medical care, there had to be a way for them to communicate to hospital staff.

One reason so many Chinese and Chinese Americans worked at the shipyards was that the Chinese community was deeply concerned about the progress of the war in the Far East. Many had fled their homeland to avoid the bloodshed that had started long before the formal outbreak of World War II. China had been an early victim of particularly brutal Japanese aggression, but now, with the help of Allied supplies, was carrying on an effective battle to free the country from the invaders. Many of these shipyard workers knew that their families and friends in China were suffering severely. Building ships was a way for American Chinese to help beat back the Imperial Japanese Army.

China's Ships

Each day at shift changes, transbay ferries carried groups of Chinese workers from San Francisco's Chinatown to the yards. Many of them worked together in crews led by an English-speaker who helped coordinate their efforts with other workers. Those who spoke no English held mostly janitorial positions cleaning up work sites, helping to keep them safe and orderly. Many others, often well-educated either in the United States or in China, worked in skilled positions in the shipways and offices. Mrs. Chow's husband was an engineer at the Kaiser yards.

When the U.S. government agreed to turn over two new Liberty ships, to be named the *Chung Shen* and the *Chung Chang*, to the Chinese government as part of the Lend-Lease program, Richmond, perhaps because of the number of Chinese workers employed there, was selected to supply them. It was good news for China because the new ships meant more supplies would soon be on their way across the Pacific. As was often the case with ships from Kaiser shipyards, these two Liberties were built even faster than called for in the already optimistic production schedule.

In the fall of 1943, when the Chinese sailors and their officers arrived to take over these brand-new vessels and put them into their country's service, the shipyard published a special issue of *Fore 'N' Aft*, to recognize Chinese-American contributions to the impressive achievements of the Richmond yards. Articles featured many of the Chinese people who had worked on the construction of these ships.

Artwork detail from the October 1, 1943 issue of Fore 'N' Aft.

Postscript: Following the war, Mr. Chow left his job at the shipyard and for the next several decades the Chows received their health care through another plan paid for by his new employer. Many decades later, Mrs. Chow, who by then was a widow, decided to switch back to Kaiser. Her application asked if she had ever been a member before. Dutifully, she wrote down that in the early 1940s, back in the shipyard days, she had been. She was surprised when her membership card arrived to learn that her medical records, well over a half-century old, had been located and that she had been assigned the same medical records number she had used so many years before!

SS Red Oak Victory

The Launching of the SS Red Oak Victory:
The Pride of an Iowa Town, and the Pride of a Shipyard

Several times now, I've had the opportunity to visit the town of Red Oak, Iowa, the place that gave its name to the only ship of the nearly 1,500 that came out of Kaiser's shipyards in Richmond and Washington-Oregon that is to be preserved. The story of the naming of that ship is related to one of the most moving accounts of the sacrifices of any town in the United States. With the help of local Iowa historians as well as the people who lived these stories, I have put together this small tribute.

Red Oak, Iowa, and the Red Oak Victory

Kaiser shipyard workers had every reason to take pride in their accomplishments. Their hard work and constant innovations made it possible to build more ships, in less time, than had ever been done in the history of the world—a total of 1,490. The Kaiser workforce built all sorts of vessels, freighters, troop carriers, and tankers as well as a variety of warships, including fifty "Kaiser" aircraft carriers. More than six decades later, ships all over the world are still being built using techniques which that workforce pioneered. The workers turned Henry Kaiser's companies into some of the most valuable assets of wartime America.

Of that great armada of nearly fifteen hundred ships built by the Kaiser workforce during World War II, only one is left to represent the literally millions of people who constructed and sailed

The deck house of the Red Oak Victory *as it looked when the ship was rescued from the Mothball Fleet in Suisun Bay in September 1998.*

Image at right: View aft from the officers' deck.

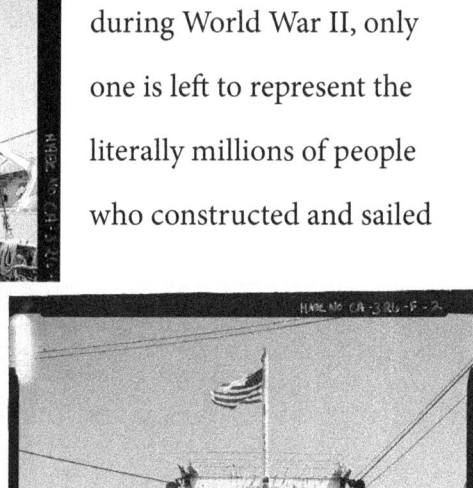

these vessels during one of the most critical periods in world history. That ship is the *SS Red Oak Victory*. To stand alongside this one ship at the dock in Richmond, California, dwarfed by the gray hull towering above you, the giant welded plates stretching out 450 feet in front of you, is probably the best way of getting a sense of the immensity of the accomplishment of the Kaiser workforce.

Looking forward from the flying bridge.

On November 9, 1944, at 10:00 a.m., Edna Reiley, wife of the mayor of Red Oak, Iowa, smashed a bottle of champagne against the brightly draped, gray steel bow. It was just three months after construction had begun. As the champagne splattered, the brand-new vessel slipped into the waters of San Francisco Bay to begin a career that would ultimately include serving in three wars.*

Launch of the SS Red Oak Victory, *November 9, 1944.*
Edna Reiley, wife of the mayor of Red Oak, Iowa, was the ship's sponsor. The ship was named to commemorate the Iowa town's wartime sacrifices.

---

* Coincidentally, this all took place only a few hundred yards from where she is now berthed. There a crew of hundreds of volunteers has been working for the past several years to get the ship ready to go to sea again, this time as a museum ship.

The *SS Red Oak Victory* carries the name of a small town founded in the middle of the nineteenth century on the rich, black soil of southwestern Iowa's Montgomery County. Almost a century later, the town earned the right to have a ship named after it because of the residents' dedication, courage, and heartbreak.

The town of Red Oak came to national attention May 3, 1943, in a *Life* magazine article: "WAR HITS RED OAK: A small Prairie town gets word that 23 of its boys are missing in action after a battle in North Africa." The article described how several weeks earlier, Rommel's Afrika Korps, battlewise and confident, had attacked American forces at places with strange-sounding names like Kasserine and Faid, somewhere in Tunisia, North Africa. There, on the edge of the Sahara Desert, the first major battle of the war between German and American forces had been fought. A powerful Afrika Korps had pushed the Americans back. Before the advance of the German Panzer divisions led by tanks had been stopped, they had engulfed an entire infantry company. That was Company M of the Iowa National Guard. In that single action, twenty-three boys from Red Oak were listed as "missing in action." In a town with a population of only 5,600, the loss was stunning. Everyone in Red Oak had known several of the missing boys.

What had happened at those two remote mountain passes, Faid and Kasserine, would bring the war to Red Oak with grief that touched every household, but, because of military secrecy, back in Iowa they wouldn't learn of it until weeks later.

This was not the first time that the men of Red Oak, fired by duty, pride, and purpose, had gone off to war. In 1861, only fifteen years after Iowa had joined the Union, the little farming town had sent volunteers to the far-off battlefields of the Civil War to help preserve it. Men from Red Oak also fought in the Spanish-American War. A generation later they were taking part in that half-forgotten 1916-1917 border war with Mexico. They had also sailed across the ocean to France to serve in the trenches to help stop the German advance on the Western Front during World War I.

It was no surprise that twenty years later, when the world went back to war, Red Oak was called on once more to pay a blood fee for freedom. To better understand how one small town could have paid such a high price in a single battle, I looked for answers at the Montgomery County Historical Society. The late Bettie McKenzie, president of its museum, pulled out old files, newspaper clippings, books and oral histories to help me in my search.

From the archived papers Bettie McKenzie gave to me to read, I learned why so many fathers, sons, husbands, brothers and sweethearts of Red Oak had been casualties of this one battle. The reason had its roots in the economics of farming during the Great Depression. Mid-America had been hit early and hard by the Depression. Service in the state militia was a small but dependable source of cash at a time and in a place where cash was very scarce. Young men from the town joined up to supplement their families' income.

The men of Company M (168th Infantry Regiment, 34th "Red Bull" Division) would meet once a week at the local armory for training. In return, they received a much-needed although modest one-dollar payment for each session. Sometimes these training sessions were quite informal. Often the citizen-soldiers would march from the armory to the nearby town square where they would practice close-order drill and run through their skirmishing tactics while curious townspeople looked on.

One former member of Company M recalled that a strong sense of urgency did not always prevail during these prewar, Depression-era training sessions. By chance, I had struck up a conversation with him over breakfast at a local hotel. When he learned that I was interested in Company M, he told me of a time when the town was being bothered by flocks of ravens roosting in the trees of the square. On the next militia evening, he and his comrades-in-arms marched to the square with shotguns they had been issued at the armory. At the order from their captain, they blasted away. The birds never returned.

However, even with their sometimes relaxed approach towards military training, state militias were the closest thing to a reserve force the U.S. Army had available at that time. On February 10, 1940, ten months before Pearl Harbor, as international tensions mounted, President Roosevelt mobilized reserve units across the nation, including the Iowa State militia. The citizen-soldiers thought that they were being called up for no more than twelve months, but events overtook such planning. They would remain in service through the end of the war.

Company M and the rest of the Red Bull Division, of which they were a part, went to Camp Claiborne in Louisiana for preparedness training in case the United States should have to enter the European war. Because the Army couldn't yet supply them with weapons, they had to make do on their maneuvers with substitutes such as stovepipes for mortars. Then, when war did break out, because they were available, the men of the Red Bull Division were among the first U.S. troops to see action.

On that February morning in 1940, as Company M marched from the Red Oak armory to the railway station, many watching were worried that their young men were heading into harm's way. But it would have taken a terrible pessimist to think that before Company M would return, the casualties would be so many that they would catapult the little town into the national news.

Three years later, a few weeks after the battles at Kasserine and Faid, the cost of the war began emerging. The evening of March 6, 1943, was a terrible time for the families of Red Oak. Telegrams from the U.S. War Department began to arrive at the local Western Union office. Each began: "The Secretary of War desires me to express his deep regret that your son has been missing in action." By midnight, more than two dozen telegrams had arrived.

A reporter for the *Saturday Evening Post* later described that day in a magazine article:

> *The news swept through Red Oak that something had happened to Company M, for all the telegrams named the National Guardsmen who had marched off so proudly only [three] years before. Families of the men in Company M gathered in the lobby of the Hotel Johnson. Someone suggested that the story of a disaster in Tunisia, which had been brushed over lightly in the Red Oak newspaper only a few weeks before, might have something to do with the telegrams. They remembered the story vaguely—how American troops had been overrun at a place called Faid Pass by a powerful German tank force.*

Among the oral histories stored in the Montgomery Country Historical Society at Red Oak are firsthand memories of the battle survivors. They are filled with stories of ingenuity and extraordinary courage told in a matter-of-fact way. One former infantryman described how he had been with a group of men who had been cut off by the German advance. After nightfall, the soldiers had realized that their only chance of making it back to their own lines was to somehow get through to the other side of a tank park where the Panzers had hunkered down until morning. The Iowans, desperate to rejoin their unit, formed into what looked like a Wermacht platoon and tried to pass themselves off in the darkness as German soldiers, even copying their marching style. They were challenged once or twice, rather half-heartedly, by tired German soldiers who seemed ready to believe that only German infantrymen would be marching through the center of their encampment. The Guardsmen had almost made it to the other side of the tank park when a German sentry, who did not get an answer to his routine challenge, opened fire. The Iowans ran. Most of them made it through to safety.

Another survivor described how he had been chased across the desert sand by several German soldiers. He had come to the top of a steep sand dune. Remembering the winters of his childhood in Red Oak sliding down snow-covered hills on the sides of cardboard boxes, he took off his knapsack and slid on it down the dune, rapidly increasing the distance between him and his pursuers. As a result, he was able to return safely to his unit.

In the months after the battle at Faid and Kasserine Pass, the people in Red Oak learned that most of the men reported missing in action were prisoners of war, but, as the war ground on, the telegrams kept coming, and the news was rarely good. A few years later, Horace Cloud, who had been a wartime mayor of Red Oak, recalled that when those first telegrams came in 1943, "we seemed to get closer together. But as bad as it was when those telegrams came, we didn't know how bad it could get." New telegrams told of young men wounded or dead all over the world: in the North Atlantic convoys, at Monte Cassino, on the beaches of Normandy, at Okinawa, Iwo Jima, at Kwajalein, and in the air over Germany. One casualty was Tom Jentoft who died aboard the *Liscome Bay*, a Kaiser-built carrier, sunk by a Japanese submarine during the invasion of the Gilbert Islands.

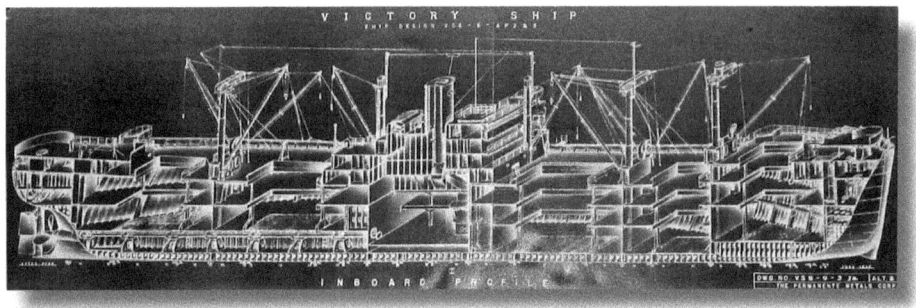

Billie Smaha, then sixteen years old, and a Western Union delivery boy, described to a reporter what his job was like, carrying the dreaded telegrams from the War Department to homes around Red Oak.

> *It was always the same when I'd get to a house. Like last winter when I went up Prospect Street to Mrs. Harold Simpson's. She came to the door when I rang and when she saw me with that telegram she turned white. I told her it wasn't good news but she was already opening the telegram and I had to help her sit down. Then her two kids came into the room and she looked at them and she said, "Your daddy is dead." That's all she said. And when I asked her if there was anything I could do, she just kept shaking her head, and I left.*

By the time the Japanese surrendered in Tokyo Bay, Billie and the other telegraph boys had delivered one hundred of the dreaded yellow envelopes, fifty of them with the three stars on the outside meaning that they carried news of the death of a loved one. A reporter figured out that for its size, Red Oak had lost more men than any city or town of its size in America. He calculated that "if New York City had lost as many sons as this Iowa town, the dead would have numbered 70,000." While some people have quibbled over exact percentages, there is no doubt that Red Oak represents the strong streak of patriotism and duty that runs through the American heartland.

Postscript: The people of Red Oak are determined that the sacrifices their veterans have made in the 150 years since their men first marched off to war will not be forgotten. A few years ago I arrived in Red Oak shortly after Memorial Day. In the cemetery were over one thousand flags on the graves of veterans placed by the people of a town that refuses to forget the courage and the sacrifices its young people have made.

The Red Oak Victory is slightly larger, better built, and far faster than the better-known Liberty ship. Liberties were designed as "emergency vessels," part of a simple but necessary strategy in the early days of the war. Those gallant but vulnerable ships and their crews were sent out to overwhelm the German submarine Atlantic blockade that was threatening to strangle Great Britain. Putting more Liberties to sea than the U-boats could sink was a bloody strategy that has been compared to trying to put out a fire by throwing more logs on it.

The Victory ship fleet, however, was a product of a later time when the balance of the war was beginning to shift in favor of the Allies. More time and money could be put into this new class of ship. Victories were bigger, three to four times more powerful, and far faster. They were designed to be, and were, the backbone of the American Merchant Marine after the war.

Vital Statistics

Typical Victory Ship

Length: 455 feet, 3 inches
Beam: 62 feet
Draft: 28 feet
Dead weight tonnage: 7,612 tons
Crew: 62 including Armed Guard
Speed: 15-17 knots (17-20 mph)
Cruising range: 23,000 miles
(The distance around the world at the equator is 24,900 miles.)

Typical Liberty ship

Length: 441 feet, 6 inches
Beam: 56 feet, 10-3/4 inches
Draft: 27 feet, 9-1/4 inches
Dead weight tonnage: 7,000 tons
Crew: 65-70 including Armed Guard
Speed: 11 to 11.5 knots (13 mph)
Cruising range: 17,000 miles

Both Liberty and Victory ships could carry similar loads in terms of weight and size. They were loaded with hundreds, if not thousands, of different kinds of materiel on their outward-bound voyages. A single ship could carry nearly 3,000 jeeps, 440 light tanks, 230 million rounds of rifle ammunition, or enough C-rations to feed 10,000 men for nine months.

The Permanente Flag

Despite the speed with which ships were turned out by Kaiser's shipyards, HJK insisted that each launching be treated as a special event. One of the rituals of Permanente Shipyards launches was the display of the Permanente flag on the gaily draped bow of the ship. Although there are many pictures of the flag taken from a distance, it proved difficult to find a clear rendition of the Permanente banner. However, with the help of Donald Bastin, former director of the Richmond Museum of History, I did find one. It is published here, perhaps for the first time in more than a half-century.

Usually, creators of flags assign meanings to each element of their design, but unfortunately, at least for now, some of the symbolism of the Permanente flag remains hidden. While the meanings of the "P," the ship, and the whirley crane (which was an essential part of Kaiser shipbuilding technique) are obvious, it is harder to know what special symbolism might be attached to the red, green, and white colors and to the colorful triangle containing the black circle. Perhaps, just as the number of stripes in the U.S. flag stands for the original thirteen states, the seven stripes on this flag stand for the seven Kaiser shipyards.

Christmas in the Shipyards

While going through a Christmas edition of *Fore 'N' Aft*, I came across the following article. The writer was John Delgado. He had started as a shipfitter in Yard No. 1 and had been promoted to leaderman before joining the staff of *Fore 'N' Aft*. He was also the chief shop steward of the Office Workers' Union. Delgado's article seems to capture the bittersweet feelings of a wartime Christmas around the world—a comparison of the warm, sentimental moments of Christmas to the grim, gritty reality of the fighting going on across the globe with the hope that the war will lead to a lasting peace.

Toward the one goal: Peace on Earth - by John Delgado

Silent night, holy night

. . . In Richmond the *chipper's guns* are stilled, the incessant honking of the whirleys is silenced, a ghostly hush replaces the clang of steel striking steel, of death and destruction. In brightly lighted homes, in crowded trailers, in spacious or dingy flats and apartments, weary war workers pause for a moment and wonder.

All is calm, all is bright

. . . On *Leyte* a screeching, whining, shuddering siren tears open the night. Pinpoints of light from cigarettes are stomped out. Someone unnecessarily warns, "They're coming again!!" … Near the River Rhine, hundreds of heavy artillery pieces roar out suddenly. Bone-tired, unshaven, gaunt men crawl through the slush and snow and blackness toward a row of pillboxes. . . . Around Budapest is forged a ring of steel that may erupt to tear men into little pieces or that may hold to entrap them until they surrender or die of starvation and thirst and disease.

Round yon Virgin, mother and child

. . . In China, a still-young woman whose face is ageless and wrinkled kneels silently beside a straw pallet, emotion betrayed only in sloe-black eyes . . . In Russia, the light from an ikon makes a halo on the blonde hair of a little boy whose father will not return from *Stalingrad*. . . . In America, in Greece, in Poland, in France, all over the world, there will be moments of sadness and prayer for the absent.

Holy infant so tender and mild

. . . A young man in camouflaged uniform darts at a sentry and with a deft motion breaks his neck, drops the dead body and moves forward . . . Another man, his legs shattered by flak, drags himself to an open bomb bay, parachutes thousands of feet to earth and lives to tell about it. . . . Still another aims a stream of liquid fire at other men who never again will torture or pillage.

Sleep in heavenly peace, sleep in heavenly peace

. . . In shallow graves in Africa, in the slime of the South Pacific, in the frozen plains of Russia, in the ankle-deep mud of Italy, they sleep; never to waken. Only for them, the war is over. For the rest of us this Christmas can be only a day in which to reassert our determination to pledge every ounce of strength, every bit of knowledge, every waking moment toward the one goal: Peace on earth, goodwill to all men. . . .

Glossary:

Chipper guns - *noisy tools used in the shipyard to clean the excess metal from the hundreds of miles of welds on each ship.*
Whirley - *the giant, rotating (whirling) cranes that move horizontally along the docks on oversized rails, lifting and placing huge prefabricated pieces onto the ships. They became a symbol of the shipyards.*
Leyte - *A Philippine island: site of one of the most decisive and bloodiest battles of World War II. Leyte was to serve as a springboard for the liberation of other islands in the Philippines as Allied troops moved closer to Japan.*
Stalingrad - *The German blitzkrieg attack on Russia was stopped at Stalingrad and, after a nearly two-year siege in which tens of thousands of soldiers and civilians died, the Germans were defeated. It is considered to be a turning point in the war.*

Part Three
Rosie the Riveter

Expanding labor needs on the home front and a male work force disappearing into the Armed Forces meant women were moving into formerly male occupations. The Kaiser shipyards policy was enlightened for the time, in particular providing equal pay for equal work and quality childcare. However, supervisors in most companies found it difficult to get used to the presence of women. The hints below are condensed from a guide published in the July 1943 issue of Transportation Magazine.

• If you can get them, pick young married women. They usually have more of a sense of responsibility than do their unmarried sisters; they're less likely to be flirtatious. As a rule, they need the work or they wouldn't be doing it—maybe a sick husband or one who's in the army. They still have the pep and interest to work hard and to deal with the public efficiently.

• While there are exceptions, general experience indicates that "husky" girls—those who are just a little on the heavy side—are likely to be more even-tempered and efficient than their underweight sisters.

• Give the female employee a definite day-long schedule of duties so that she'll keep busy without bothering the management for instructions every few minutes. ... Women make excellent workers when they have their jobs cut out for them, but they lack initiative in finding work themselves.

• Give every girl an adequate number of rest periods during the day. A girl has more confidence and consequently is more efficient if she can keep her hair tidied,

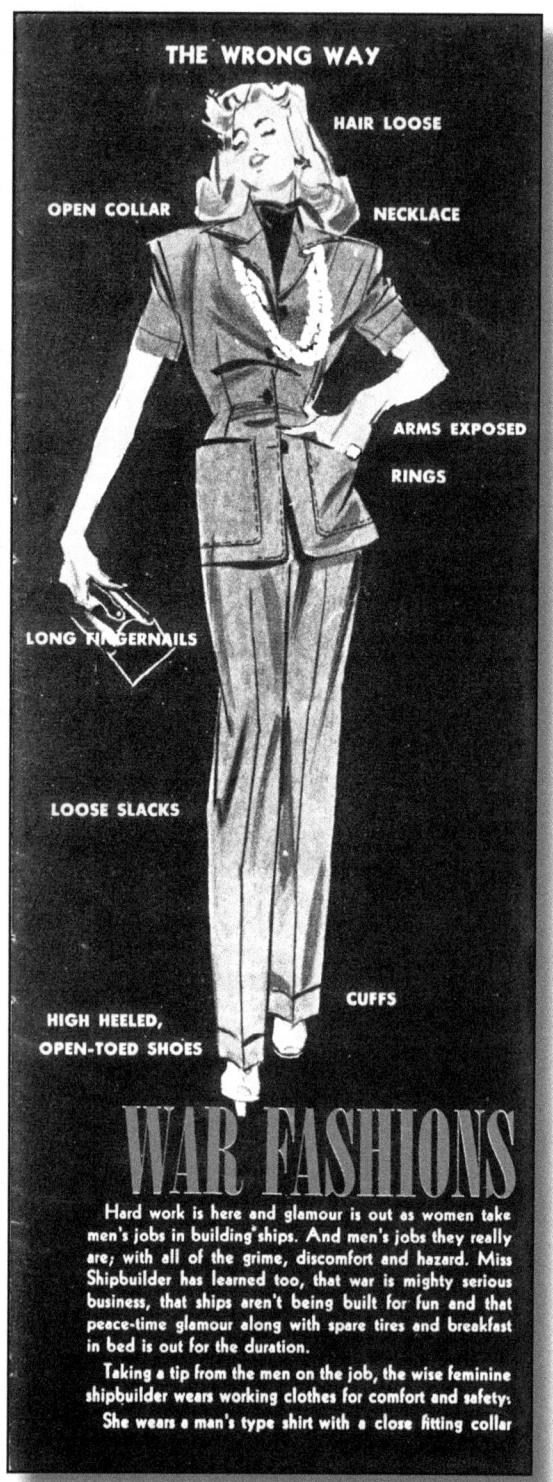

A great deal of attention was paid to the work clothes of women employed in the actual production of ships. In addition to safety reminders, there were

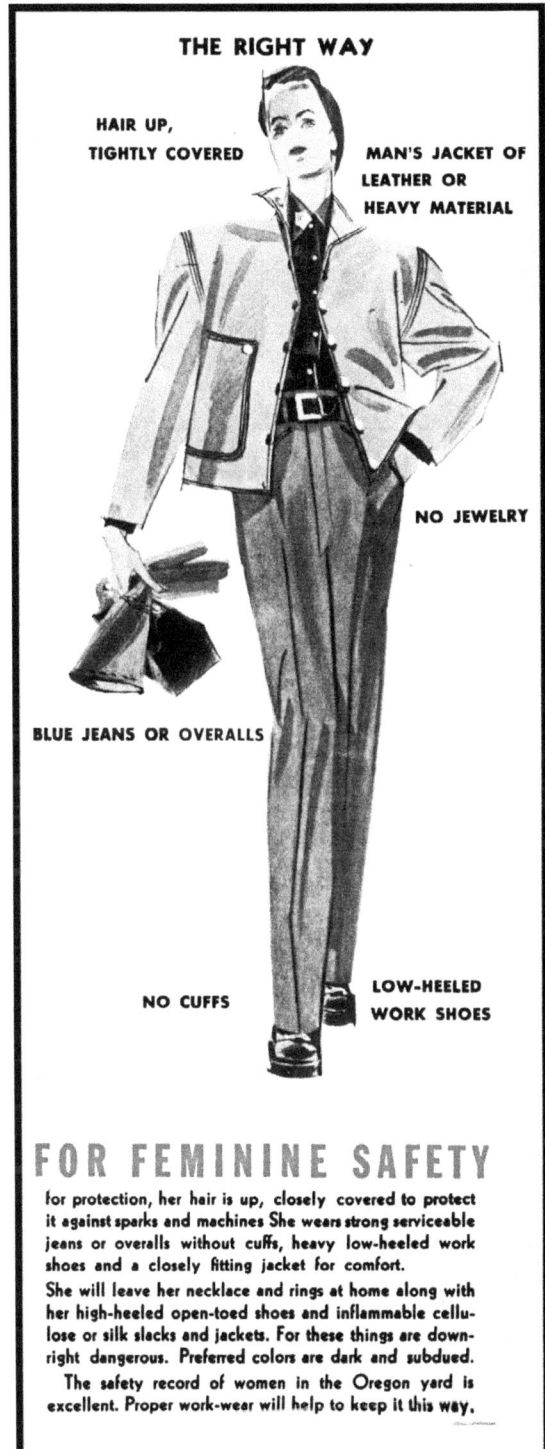

...even shipyard fashion articles featuring attractive coveralls that met all safety requirements while allowing the femininity of the worker to be expressed.

apply fresh lipstick and wash her hands several times a day.

- Be reasonably considerate about using strong language around women. Even though a girl's husband or father may swear vociferously, she'll grow to dislike a place of business where she hears too much of this.

- When you have to use older women, try to get ones who have worked outside the home at some time in their lives. . . . Older women who have never contacted the public have a hard time adapting themselves. They are inclined to be cantankerous and fussy.

- Retain a physician to give each woman you hire a special physical examination—one covering female conditions. This step not only protects the property against the possibilities of lawsuit but also reveals whether the employee-to-be has any female weaknesses, which would make her mentally or physically unfit for the job. Transit companies that follow this practice report a surprising number of women turned down for nervous disorders.

- Whenever possible, let the inside employee change from one job to another at some time during the day. Women are inclined to be nervous and they're happier with change.

- Be tactful in issuing instructions or in making criticisms. Women are often sensitive; they can't shrug off harsh words the way that men do. Never ridicule a woman—it breaks her spirit and cuts her efficiency.

How Henry J. Kaiser and the Rosies Helped Win World War II

"We Can Do It."
This is the poster commonly but erroneously named "Rosie the Riveter." It was created in 1942 by Howard Miller, a graphic artist at Westinghouse Corporation.

Pgs. 120-21: Some of Richmond's Rosies - a crew of basin shipfitters: (left to right) Alma Treick, Sally Martin, Hazel Motte, Geneva Gordon, Toni Lindly, Mary Duncan, and Hazel Harris. The caption to this Fore "N' Aftt *photograph noted that the crew introduced an innovation that reduced costs by 80%.*

Rosie the Riveter

Rosie the Riveter is one of the most enduring images of World War II. She came to represent the women on the home front who had made possible the unprecedented flow of tools of war to Allied soldiers and airmen around the world. Of the four hundred thousand or so workers who passed through the Kaiser yards, at times up to 25 percent of the workforce were women. In one yard, the number peaked at 60 percent!

Today the Rosie image is an inclusive one. She no longer symbolizes only riveters, or even just women. In a way, she has come to stand for all the home front workers but especially the six million women who played a vital part in the wartime labor force. Originally, of course, "Rosie the Riveter" had represented solely the women on the home front doing jobs that until then had been thought of as "men's work." The Rosie image continues to resonate with women today because she evokes not only an historical period but also a contemporary "We can do it!" spirit. That makes it all the more amazing that although she became a folk figure, recognized in every part of the nation, her birth was almost accidental.

For most people, the phrase "Rosie the Riveter" calls up the familiar image of a strong, confident, attractive working woman, hair bound in a red bandana, rolling up the sleeve on her flexed arm, presumably to get down to some serious physical labor. Because so many women were joining the workforce, anxious to become a part of the war effort, the concept of a "Rosie the Riveter" caught the imagination of the public. She seemed to express the positive outlook of the women themselves as they discovered that they could push back the boundaries of what was defined as "men's work." Rosie became the women's equivalent of GI Joe, representing all working women, in whatever industries, in whatever jobs. By 1943, the mass media of the day, newsreels, radio broadcasts, magazines, and newspapers, were all looking for their own Rosie the Riveter. The enthusiasm of the media for the phrase has led to speculation about whether a "real" Rosie existed, and if so, whom might she be. The search for her turned out to be an interesting one with more than a few surprises.

Before beginning our search, though, it would be useful to know a little about riveting, what it is, and how it's done. Riveting is a way of fastening steel plates together. A rivet is a short metal rod with a head at one end. It is heated until it is red hot. Then it is driven through specially cut holes in the two pieces of steel that are to be joined. While the rivet is still red hot and malleable, the other end is hammered so it spreads over the hole, holding the two parts together. Sybil Lewis, an African-American wartime riveter for Lockheed Aircraft in Los Angeles described the process this way:

A selection of steel rivets.

> *The women worked in pairs. I was the riveter and this big, strong, white girl from a cotton farm in Arkansas worked as the "bucker." The riveter used a gun to shoot rivets through the metal and fasten it together. The bucker used a bucking bar on the other side of the metal to smooth out the rivets. Bucking was harder than shooting rivets; it required more muscle. Riveting required more skill.*

The Familiar Rosie

The image that most people today associate with Rosie was created in 1942 by J. Howard Miller, a graphic artist at Westinghouse Corporation. At the time the federal government was encouraging industries to recruit women to combat a serious labor shortage as more and more able-bodied men were being siphoned out of the labor force into the military. The poster, part of a series created by Miller, was Westinghouse's contribution. But that "We Can Do It" Rosie originally had nothing to do with either Rosies or riveting. The image conveyed an anonymous woman doing a nonspecific job. Her purpose was to encourage women to go out and take jobs in the war industries. The poster was originally not seen outside of Westinghouse, where it was on view for only two weeks before being replaced by the next poster in the Miller series. The "We Can Do It" poster would remain in semi-obscurity for almost thirty years before finding a new life as a symbol of the women's movement of the 1970s. In 1984, the U.S. Post Office released a postage stamp featuring the now familiar working woman.

However, if this woman was not Rosie, who was she? Long after the poster's creation, two women have been associated with the image. In 2002 Ethel Kelly toured through small towns in Mississippi with the Smithsonian Institution/Humanities Councils wartime exhibit, "Produce for Victory," as the woman who had inspired J. Howard Miller's famous poster. Early in World War II, nineteen-year-old Kelly, like so many other small-town women of that time, got on a bus and headed west. She found a job at Lockheed Aviation in Burbank, California, working on the swing shift. Sixty years later, a local paper asked rhetorically, "Who would have thought that a young, newly married woman from Delhi, Louisiana, whose husband was serving in Europe, would hop a bus to Burbank, California, to work the swing shift in a plant for the war effort, would wind up being one of the most recognizable faces from the era?"

Another aircraft worker, Geraldine Hoff Doyle, however, was also convinced that she had been the model. Like Ethel Kelly, she, too had never seen the poster until it had reappeared in the 1980s. Her friends and relatives were positive they saw the resemblance, and in fact a UPI news photographer had taken a picture of her during the war. She was wearing a red bandana, operating a large metal lathe. When Mrs. Doyle passed away in late 2010, the *New York Times* referred to her as the inspiration for the famous face on the poster.

Rosie Becomes a Household Name, and Steps into History

As ubiquitous as it may be, the "We Can Do It" poster marks a false start in the search for the "real" Rosie the Riveter. Perhaps the real beginning, the birthday, if you had to pick one, for Rosie the Riveter, was Friday, January 15, 1943, in Chicago. On that date, a popular quartet calling themselves the "Four Vagabonds" went into a studio to record two songs they had rehearsed for this session. There was a hitch, though. At the last minute, the composer of the songs refused to give them permission to record his tunes, and it looked as though the session would be canceled.

Although the Vagabonds were a well-known group with fan clubs from coast-to-coast, unlike the other big stars of the time, they didn't do much recording. Instead, they concentrated on live appearances on radio. With an astounding fifteen hundred songs in their repertoire, great flexibility, and an acknowledged ability to prepare new songs quickly, they were always in demand. They had been singing together for almost ten years and had perfected their harmonies to blend their voices into a single, smooth stream of melodic sound. By 1943, they were regulars on the ABC Radio Network and best known nationally for their daily appearances on the very popular, hour-long, five-morning-a-week, Don McNeil's Breakfast Club, where they sang three songs each broadcast and participated in the on-air comedy, which was a part of each show.

On this particular day when the four singers went to the RCA Victor Company's Chicago recording studio and learned that the songs they had worked up could not be recorded, they must have been disappointed. Their agreement with the Bluebird label, a subsidiary of RCA Victor, promised $3,000 for each recording session. Perhaps that is why, when the record company executives approached them with sheet music for two substitute songs, they agreed to look them over on the spot. They spent some time with the music, experimenting with the harmonies, to see how they might perform the songs. Confident that they could do it, they told the record producers that if they could have one hour more to work on the arrangements for the two songs, they would be ready to record "Rose of Charing Cross" and "Rosie the Riveter."

"Rosie" had been written several months earlier by two established songwriters, Redd Evans and John Jacob Loeb.[*] Their inspiration had been a 1942 newspaper column describing how Rosalind Palmer, a recent high school graduate, had taken a job at an aircraft factory near New York City where, as a riveter, she was helping to assemble the beautiful but deadly Corsair fighter planes for the U.S. Navy. The columnist dubbed her "Rosie the Riveter."

---

[*]Redd Evans had already written "There, I've Said It Again," which had been recorded by several well-known artists but wouldn't become a classic until it was recorded by Vaughn Monroe later in 1943. Coincidentally, Loeb later collaborated with Carmen Lombardo on several hits recorded by Carmen's brother Guy and his band, including the Arthur Godfrey theme, "Seems like Old Times." Guy Lombardo was also an outstanding racing hydroplane driver who often raced successfully in big-time international Unlimited Hydroplane competitions for the man most closely associated with the "Rosie the Riveter" image, Henry Kaiser.

Evans and Loeb had been intrigued by the sound and naturally syncopated rhythm of the words "Rosie the Riveter" and by the contrast between the floral associations of the name and the deadly serious nature of the industrial process Rosie was engaged in. When they had finished writing their new piece, they had little trouble convincing the Bluebird Record Company to buy it. Unfortunately, once the record company had purchased it, they had just let the music sit in a filing cabinet until that January morning. It was the unexpected refusal of an unknown songwriter to release his music to the Four Vagabonds that sent the company executives scurrying to their file cabinets to find a replacement. That was the day that Rosie the Riveter stepped into her place in history.

The recording that created a timeless icon.

When the Four Vagabonds stepped up to the microphone to record, they nailed each of the songs on the first take. When you listen to their delightful and complex arrangement of "Rosie," complete with sound effects made by the singers, you can appreciate their achievement. "Rosie the Riveter," almost overlooked, appropriately enough had been discovered in an emergency and had begun her career by setting a production record.

The song was released the next month and was an immediate hit. People recognized in this Rosie the spirit that had led their daughters, sisters, wives, and sweethearts to go out into the workplace to do "men's jobs" as their way of participating in the war effort.

Rosie the Riveter

All the day long,

Whether rain or shine,

She's a part of the assembly line.

She's making history,

Working for victory,

Rosie, the Riveter.

Keeps a sharp lookout for sabotage,

Sitting up there on the fuselage.

That little frail can do

More than a male can do.

Rosie, the Riveter.

Rosie's got a boyfriend, Charlie.

Charlie, he's a Marine.

Rosie is protecting Charlie,

Working overtime on the riveting machine.

When they gave her a production "E,"

She was as proud as a girl could be.

There's something true about,

Red, white, and blue about,

Rosie, the Riveter.

While the song played out over millions of radios and Victrolas across the nation, Rosalind Palmer, the young woman whose story had inspired the songwriters, continued working at the aircraft manufacturing plant, quietly avoiding the local publicity she had generated as the socialite working for the war effort.

The "Rosie" Who Started It All

In 2007, I spoke with Rosalind Palmer. Today she lives in New York City and is active on a national level in the promotion of her lifelong interest in social justice. She is a vigorous supporter of educational, cultural, and social organizations that promote such efforts and is on the boards of several of these organizations. She described to me her wartime career as a riveter, how the Rosie story had come about, and why she has chosen to keep a low profile.

When Rosalind graduated from a Connecticut high school in June 1942, six months had elapsed since the Japanese attack on Pearl Harbor. Each day's newspaper described the progress of a war that stretched across the globe as America organized on both the battlefields and the home front to defeat the Axis attackers. Young Rosalind, though, was looking forward to a summer of tennis and swimming at the local country club. She told me that her father, president of a major pharmaceutical company, put a stop to that: "There's a war going on. Go do something to help." At his insistence, she found a way to contribute to the war effort. She got her chance when she was hired by the aircraft manufacturing company, Vought-Sikorsky Corporation. At their Stratford, Connecticut plant, where they were manufacturing the beautiful, but deadly, Corsair, a Navy fighter plane, they had only recently begun hiring women for production work on what was generally agreed to be one of the finest military aircraft ever built. Although there was a great deal of skepticism among male workers and even some mild hostility, the newly-hired Palmer was assigned to learn riveting.

Fortunately, the foreman selected to train her, Charlie Primavera, believed that women were capable of doing the job well, and he took her training seriously. Unfortunately, she got off to a bad start—"I drove a hole in Charlie's finger"—but under his supervision, she became proficient in her new trade.

Rosalind started on the graveyard shift, 6:30 in the evening to 5:30 the next morning. For her first assignment she worked as a "bucker" on aircraft wings. A bucker is one-half of a two-person riveting team. When holes drilled through the material to be fastened were lined up for riveting, the bucker held a metal bar firmly on the interior side. A rivet, driven by the riveter's pneumatic gun, would be smashed against the bucker's bar, flattening the head so that it couldn't move back through the hole, thus holding the metal plates together.

An important part of the bucker's responsibility was to fashion her own bars to fit inside the tight spaces within the aircraft wing where the pneumatic gun would pound a rivet. As more plates were fastened onto the wing, the working area for the bucker became more and more closed-up. Placing the bar exactly behind the next rivet became increasingly difficult. Rosalind introduced an improvement to this process that, not surprisingly, had not occurred to the men. She would reach up into the wing, at times up to her shoulder, holding the mirror of her compact to see the next place where she needed to place her bucker's bar.

Meanwhile, her own riveting skills were increasing, and as a result, she was soon working with her own bucker. The two of them developed such a good reputation that before long Rosalind was promoted to lead riveter working on the wing and air ducts of the Corsairs.

Rosalind's father was the president of the Squibb Company, one of the nation's largest drug manufacturers. The Palmer family was prominent in the Bridgeport, Connecticut area as well as in New York. When word reached the society editor of the *Bridgeport Herald* that Palmer's daughter was working as a riveter at the nearby aircraft plant, he printed the news as yet another example of how people from all parts of society were pitching in to help the war effort.

The next step in the creation of Rosie the Riveter came about when that local story caught the attention of the *New York Journal-American* syndicated society reporter who wrote under the pen-name of Cholly Knickerbocker. The Knickerbocker column was widely popular, not just because it chronicled the doings of the rich and famous, but also because he did it in an amusing style. Knickerbocker had a knack for adding entertaining detail and, especially, for phrasemaking. A number of his creations, including "glamour girl" and "café society," are still in common use.

The item he saw in the Bridgeport paper about young socialite Rosalind Palmer working as a riveter at the Sikorsky plant suggested to him another phrase. It would outshine all his others, although no one could have guessed this when he typed "Rosie the Riveter" into the copy for that day's column. The phrase would take on a life of its own.

Rosalind's first reaction to seeing her name in Cholly Knickerbocker's society column was embarrassment. She had wanted to be just another one of the workers at the plant doing her part to defeat Japan and Germany. Now her coworkers knew about her family background. It made her feel conspicuous and awkward, but she discovered that those feelings passed. Because of her energy, enthusiasm, and the quality of her work, she was soon accepted for herself and for her work on the production line.

She was a good riveter. Rosalind had started out as one of about ten women working in the aircraft plant, but the increasing need for workers meant that more were being hired. In order to determine whether or not they should be paid at the same rate as men, the company wanted to learn whether women could place as many rivets in the same amount of time as men did. Palmer was selected for testing. In true Rosie style, she showed that she was doing better work than many of the men. That was what the company wanted to know, and, very appropriately, they adopted a policy of equal pay for the women.

Oddly enough, no one at the aircraft plant ever called Rosalind "Rosie"; she was always "Roz." She had never even been called Rosie at home or at school. In fact the woman who was the inspiration for an icon that continues to inspire millions was only called Rosie that one time. When I asked her why it was that she chose to keep a low profile all of these years, her answer was both modest and understandable. She has never tried to keep her Rosie connection hidden, but neither has she advertised it. She has always felt that, as interesting as it was, it was an accident of fate, not something that she had earned. She had done no more than hundreds of thousands of other "Rosies" had done during World War II and feels that any personal publicity around her would detract from the achievements of the other women of that great women's production army in which she, too, had served.

That Knickerbocker column and the song it inspired led to the creation of still other "Rosies," many in the spring and summer of 1943.

Walter Pidgeon, a handsome and distinguished Canadian actor, was one of the most popular Hollywood figures of the day. During the war, he undertook a campaign of personal appearances around the United States and sold more than five million dollars in war bonds. He also made a short film capitalizing on the popularity of the

Rosie the Riveter ideal. For this, he and a film crew traveled to Ypsilanti, Michigan, to the gigantic aircraft factory recently built by the Ford Company at Willow Run.*

The plant had been a mammoth undertaking, at 3.5 million square feet, the largest manufacturing facility in the world. Charles Lindbergh called it the "Grand Canyon of the mechanized world." It had a problem, though: not enough workers to "man" the assembly lines that were turning out the heavy bombers needed on the fighting fronts of the world. To remedy this, the government had ordered Ford to hire and train women so that by the time the Hollywood crew arrived, there were thousands of women working there, many of them riveters. One was Rose Will Monroe, a widowed mother raising two daughters by herself. She was independent of spirit, attractive, poised, and articulate. She became the Rosie of the film Walter Pidgeon was preparing.

Several years ago, one of Rose Monroe's daughters told the story of how her mother, although not the woman in the "We Can Do It" poster, came to be associated with the image of Rosie.

Rose Will Monroe, the Rosie who was "discovered" by Hollywood screen idol, Walter Pidgeon.

Mom happened to be in the right place at the right time. . . . Mom never posed for any posters or paintings. She only appeared in war bond promotional movies with the British [sic] actor Walter Pidgeon to help finance the war effort. Mr. Pidgeon came to her factory to film the promos, and Mom's foreman said he had a worker named Rose, who was a riveter and fit the stereotype of the "Rosie" of the popular song of the day. After getting her permission to do so, she appeared in the films, totally unpaid. She supported the war effort, and this was her part in helping get our guys back home as safely and quickly as possible.

---

* After the war, this huge factory would become the home of the Kaiser automobile company.

Rosie Gets a Face

In wartime America *The Saturday Evening Post*, with a circulation of four million, could honestly call itself "America's Magazine," and covers by America's most celebrated artist, Norman Rockwell, had helped to make this so. The artist was phenomenally popular. So many people collected his covers, putting them up on walls, even framing them, that the company always published extra copies of any Rockwell issue.

For the war effort, the government had asked the help of the national magazines to sell war bonds. In turn, the Post had commissioned Rockwell to create a cover with a woman worker as a subject. His "Rosie the Riveter" was a brawny, somewhat grimy worker so vigorous, powerful, and motivated that on her lunch break she eats her sandwich with her heavy riveting gun resting on her rather substantial lap. The "Rosie" cover is filled with wonderful detail. Instead of placing his model on a proverbial pedestal, Rockwell has chosen to seat her on a more down-to-earth industrial crate of some sort. The front of

With the help of Michelangelo, Norman Rockwell created the first image of Rosie the Riveter.

her blue denim coveralls has a line of pins and buttons. It is her "jewelry" and shows that she is an active participant in the war effort in more ways than just her work: she has given blood, bought war bonds, and most prominent among these pins is her ID badge with her picture on it. It is a symbol of official recognition that she definitely belongs in the workplace.

Despite her sturdy physique and powerful biceps, Rosie retains her femininity. The smudges she has accumulated on her face during her shift do not hide her makeup and lipstick. This moment of lunchtime relaxation is only momentary. She hasn't even bothered to remove her burn goggles or her face shield. Part of the shield is flipped up out of the way over the top of her head and it looks a bit like a halo, as though she were the patron saint of production. Behind her, the backdrop of a huge American flag suggests that this is the patriotic portrait of a home front secular saint of patriotism. Her feet, clad in low-cut shoes, loafers or moccasins, rest matter-of-factly on a discarded copy of Adolf Hitler's manifesto, *Mein Kampf*.

One historian has written of an unintended, but illuminating meaning of those shoes: "Only after July 1943 were safety shoes with metal toes produced for women. There had been no need to manufacture these shoes in women's sizes before, because women didn't customarily work in dangerous jobs where such shoes were needed. Most women wore their own shoes." Rosies were treading on new ground.

There were actually two models for this powerful woman on the cover of that May 29, 1943 issue of the *Saturday Evening Post*. Both were unlikely. The first was Mary Doyle, a slim, attractive nineteen-year-old, who weighed in at a petite 110 pounds. She worked part-time as a telephone operator in Arlington, Vermont, where Rockwell had his studio. She was definitely not a riveter, but Rockwell often used people from town as his models. Almost everyone in Arlington had at least one friend or family member who had appeared on a *Saturday Evening Post* cover. Rockwell had found something in Mary Doyle's face that he wanted his woman war worker to express, and he invited Mary to the studio to pose for him. Doyle, whom Rockwell later said was the most beautiful woman he had ever seen, spent two mornings being photographed by Rockwell in a variety of poses, one of which he chose for the portrait. (For this she received a modeling fee of ten dollars, which was standard for the time and place.)

Mary Doyle may have had the face Rockwell needed for his portrait of the woman war worker, but she definitely did not have the powerful, larger-than-life physique that Rockwell wanted for his Rosie. For that he turned to the classics.

He found what he was looking for among the startlingly beautiful images created more than four centuries earlier by Michelangelo in the Vatican's Sistine Chapel: the Old Testament prophet Isaiah. Rockwell experimented with cutouts of Mary Doyle's head placed on reproductions of the brawny image of that prophet until he was satisfied he had found the balance he needed between femininity and power. The blending of those figures created a powerful icon that captured both the image and the reality of the millions of women who were entering the work force in jobs previously considered men's work.

From the Renaissance, an unlikely model for a World War II icon. (Compare with Rockwell Rosie on page 137).

Rockwell deliberately named his woman worker Rosie, as can be seen in the simple, white letters drawn on her black lunch box, located behind the rivet gun. Very likely he knew Evan and Loeb's enormously popular song, from the radio, which played it a great deal, or from the record, which was selling briskly. By the time Rockwell chose his subject, journalists had also picked up the phrase "Rosie the Riveter." "Rosie the Riveter" was in the air.

Today, Rockwell's Rosie is not as well-known as Miller's "We Can Do It" image, even though at the time millions of citizens saw the *Saturday Evening Post* cover. Why has the "We Can Do It" poster replaced this original Rosie image? The simple answer, in one word, is copyright. Rockwell's Rosie belonged to the owners of Curtis Publishing, the publishers of the *Saturday Evening Post*, while the Westinghouse "We Can Do It" poster, produced under the auspices of the U.S. government went into the public domain. "We Can Do It" was a powerful image, and it was available without charge. Rockwell's Rosie, however, is still treasured. An anonymous collector recently paid $4.9 million for the original painting.

A Record-Breaking Rosie

On June 8, 1943, at a Tarrytown, New York, aircraft factory, two cousins, a riveter named Rose "Rosie" Bonavita and her bucker, Jennie Fiorito, set a production record. In one shift, they drove an astonishing 3,345 rivets into the tail assembly of an Avenger torpedo bomber. For this, Rose Bonavita was immediately dubbed "Rosie the Riveter" by the press, and she received a personal letter of commendation from President Roosevelt.

Although she isn't well known to the general public, the late Ms. Bonavita's achievement has garnered some lasting fame. In a list compiled five years ago at Holy Cross College in Worcester, Massachusetts, she was named one of one hundred outstanding Italian-American women, along with actress Pier Angeli, politician Geraldine Ferraro, singer Liza Minelli, athlete Jennifer Capriatti, and even the saint, Mother Cabrini. And more than sixty years later, Rosie Bonavita's achievement still inspires. In her honor, her hometown baseball team of Cortland (New York) has chosen to call itself "The Riveters."

Rosie Goes Hollywood

As the idea of Rosie the Riveter continued to become more and more popular, it was probably inevitable that Hollywood would make a movie about her. The story that would take Rosie from the assembly line to Hollywood had been published in *The Saturday Evening Post*, April 17, 1943. "Room for Two," by Elizabeth Curnow Handley, was transformed by the author into a movie script with the very saleable title, *Rosie the Riveter*. The film, released in 1944 by Republic Pictures, starred Jane Frazee and Frank Albertson. The comedy depicts the antics of four airplane factory workers, two women and two men working on different shifts, who share a boarding house room. "Pretty silly, but harmless," noted TV Guide. Although not a classic, the film did succeed in burning the Rosie image further into the consciousness of America. Rosie was on her way to becoming a powerful, near mythic figure that would long outlast "the duration."

Richmond's Own Rosie

The cover of the March 1943 issue of Fore 'N' Aft *was one of many emphasizing the contributions of women in the Kaiser shipyards.*

In the 1990s, Donna Powers, Richmond City Councilwoman and one of the strongest supporters of the Rosie the Riveter National Park proposal, was looking for a picture of someone to represent the women workers of the shipyards. She found what she was looking for in a 1945 issue of *Fore 'N' Aft*. Powers had located a photo of an African-American shipworker who seemed to capture the vitality, confidence, and independence of the women of the wartime shipyards.

The photograph was incorporated into a poster celebrating the development of the park. A copy of the poster was placed in the window of a Richmond graphic arts shop where it set off an unexpected chain of events. Aminah Bilal happened to see the poster there, and she was stunned. "That's my grandmother," she said. The image on the poster was a photograph of Charles "Charlie" Etta Turner, taken fifty years before, when she had been a ship fitter at the Kaiser Richmond shipyards. But there was much more to the story than simple coincidence. There was romance as well.

Charlie had been taking a break that hot summer day in 1945. She'd found a welcome bit of shade beneath some iron beams and it was there that *Fore 'N' Aft* photographer Bill Turner spotted her. He'd never seen her before but decided immediately that she would be a good subject. After asking her permission, he peered through his viewfinder and took her photograph. That picture turned out to be a record of an important moment in both Bill's and Charlie's lives, because a few years later they were married, becoming, incidentally, one of the first legally-married interracial couples in California.

In 1996, more than a half-century after the photograph was taken, but in time for the dedication of the Rosie the Riveter World War II Home Front National Historical Park, the picture of "Charlie" was reproduced on seventy-five red, white, and blue banners. Ten feet high and flown from poles, the banners rimmed the new park and lined nearby streets. On Dedication Day, both men and women "Rosies" gathered on a broad lawn beside the Rosie the Riveter Memorial, on land that had once been a Kaiser shipyard, to celebrate their achievements five decades earlier and to receive the thanks of younger generations for their wartime efforts. Among the Rosies that day were Bill and Charlie Turner, who were there with their daughter, their five grandchildren, and their four great-grandchildren. After a half-century, and forty-eight years of marriage to the long-ago photographer, Charlie Turner had once again become a symbol for all the Rosies of Richmond.

Mrs. Mary Carroll was one of tens of thousands of women who flocked to the Kaiser shipyards to help in the war effort. She signed up after learning her son was missing in action in the Philippines.

Why Rosie Was a Welder

Rosie the Riveter has become such a powerful and widely-agreed-upon symbol of the home front during World War II that it is a bit surprising to realize that in the shipyards, if sheer numbers were the only yardstick, "Wendy the Welder" would actually be more appropriate. In fact, for a while during the war, "Wendy the Welder" was in common use in Northern California, because in the shipyards far more women and men were working as welders than riveters. The new method of ship construction used welding over riveting.

Traditionally, the steel plate that is fashioned into the hulls, decks, and bulkheads of ships was held together by riveting. Riveted ships are strong and they are durable, but there are disadvantages, too, particularly in the construction process. It took time and craftsmanship to align steel plates so that the holes to be drilled through each plate for the rivets would match up. Even with highly skilled drillers, the match was rarely perfect. As a result, these holes had to be enlarged by another craftsman, a "reamer," so the rivets would pass through; and the holes needed to remain small enough so the head of the rivet could clinch the plates together. Finally, with the riveter on one side of the hull and the bucker on the other, the red-hot iron pin could be driven through and the partly-molten head smashed repeatedly until both ends were flattened to hold the plate in place. The rivets on the hull also had to be smoothed by other workers so as not to slow the ship down. Production was slow and expensive.

About 150,000 rivets would be needed on a vessel roughly the size of a Liberty or Victory ship built by traditional methods, meaning at least double that number of holes to be drilled and reamed. According to some estimates, riveting added around 300 tons to the weight of the ship, cutting down by that much the amount of cargo it could carry. Welding plates together with about forty miles worth of welds instead of fastening them with 150,000 rivets seemed like an attractive alternative. But there were problems, too.

As far back as the First World War, shipyards had tried welding, but no one had yet built a ship that was essentially welded rather than riveted. However, recent advances in welding technology had opened up new possibilities. Electric arc welding had improved greatly between the wars, speeding up the welding process and making stronger joints than had been possible before that time. Now, with German submarines choking off the movement of supplies to Great Britain from the United States and Canada, there was an urgent need for new ships to be constructed as rapidly as possible.

As a result, the potential advantages of welding overwhelmed the "we have always built ships with rivets" attitude of old-time shipbuilders. If welds were done right, they could be as strong as riveted joints. Another big advantage of welding was that a skilled instructor could take a man or woman off the street and turn him or her into a capable welder with basic skills after just one or two weeks of training as opposed to riveting, which took far longer to learn. Furthermore, the preassembly method used by World War II shipbuilders, and in particular Henry Kaiser, meant that giant shipyard cranes could lift huge ship sections, turning them over as they were being fabricated so that novice welders were always working "down-hand": the seams they were joining were below them, so gravity was on their side. This is the easiest sort of welding. However, welding was far from effortless. Even getting to the job site could be a struggle.

At the beginning of each shift, welders had to pick up their heavy machines from the dockside tool sheds and, with bulky electric power cables slung over their shoulders, climb the tall ladders up the ship's hull to their workplace. One interesting feature of the Kaiser shipyards was that because climbing to the work site on a ship was often so physically demanding, shipyard management developed a training course to help women build up their strength for the climb and learn how best to carry the equipment.

However, as efficient as welding had become, shipbuilders still had some hard lessons to learn before they could take full advantage of the new technology. When the first welded ships went to sea, some of the hulls buckled, and some decks and bulkheads cracked. Several ships even sank because of welds springing open. Investigation showed that welding could build up stresses in the hull in a way that riveting did not. Sudden temperature changes such as a ship sailing into an Arctic Ocean current or the battering of stormy seas would increase the strains until a seam gave way and a crack opened up.*

Shipbuilders were quick to learn from their mistakes. With help from engineers and naval architects, new welding techniques were developed that relieved these built-in pressures. For the next twenty years the "temporary" Liberty ships with welded hulls were a common sight on the world's oceans, steaming from port-to-port, an essential part of international trade. The wartime cousins of the Liberty ships, the larger, faster Victory ships, also with welded hulls, were sturdy enough to become the backbone of the postwar American Merchant Marine fleet until the 1970s, when they were replaced by a new generation of merchant ships, containerized freighters.

---

*This cracking happened to hulls built at a number of shipyards, including Kaiser's. After the war, a federal commission investigating the quality of work done by shipbuilding contractors concluded that despite the speed with which Kaiser produced ships, quality ranked among the highest in American shipbuilding facilities.

These unidentified women shipyard workers, dressed in their leathers, helmets, and face shields seem to exhibit wonder and pride at their new roles as welders.

Kaiser's 'WINKS'

WINKS, Women in Kaiser Shipyards, was the Kaiser way of including, for recognition, all women working in the yards, from secretaries and truck drivers to welders and chippers.

In the spring of 1943, as "Rosie the Riveter" fever, in picture and in song, captured the imagination of the nation, Kaiser yards developed their own name for the women working there: WINKS, "Women in Kaiser Shipyards." They recognized that relatively few of the thousands of women working in the yards were actually riveters, but that there were tens of thousands working as welders, drivers, shipfitters, dispatchers, secretaries, burners, fire personnel, chippers, drafters and all sorts of other occupations. These women played a vital part in the record-breaking successes of the yards. The "WINKS"

Most of the welding was done with electric arc welders. However, burners, such as this unidentified woman, were so skilled in the use of oxyacetlene torches that they could burn away excess metal that would otherwise have to be chipped away much more slowly with hand chisels.

column in the weekly shipyard magazine recognized their role with stories featuring women in all of these occupations.

How Henry J. Kaiser and the Rosies Helped Win World War II

Part Four:
Kaiser Permanente

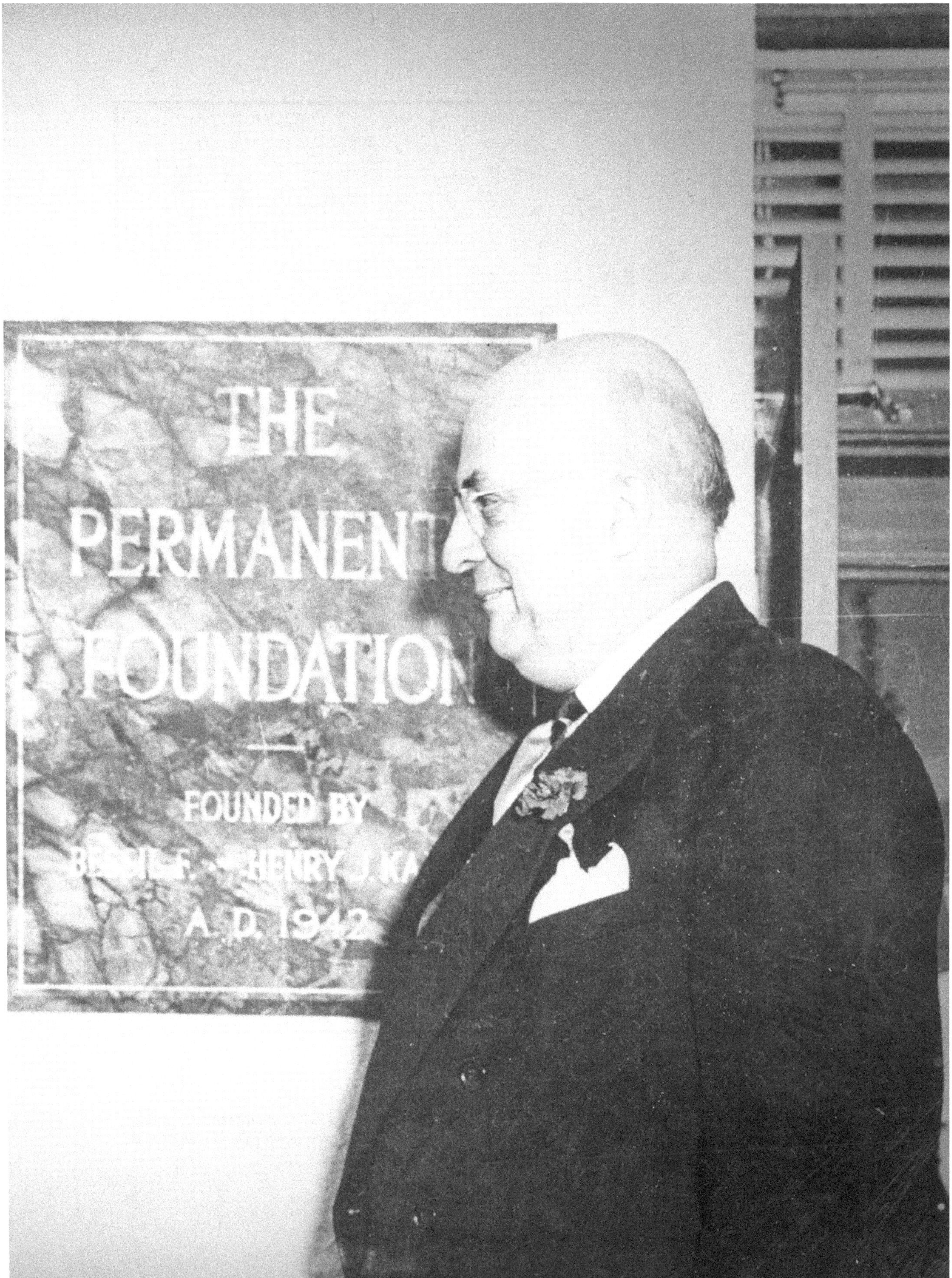

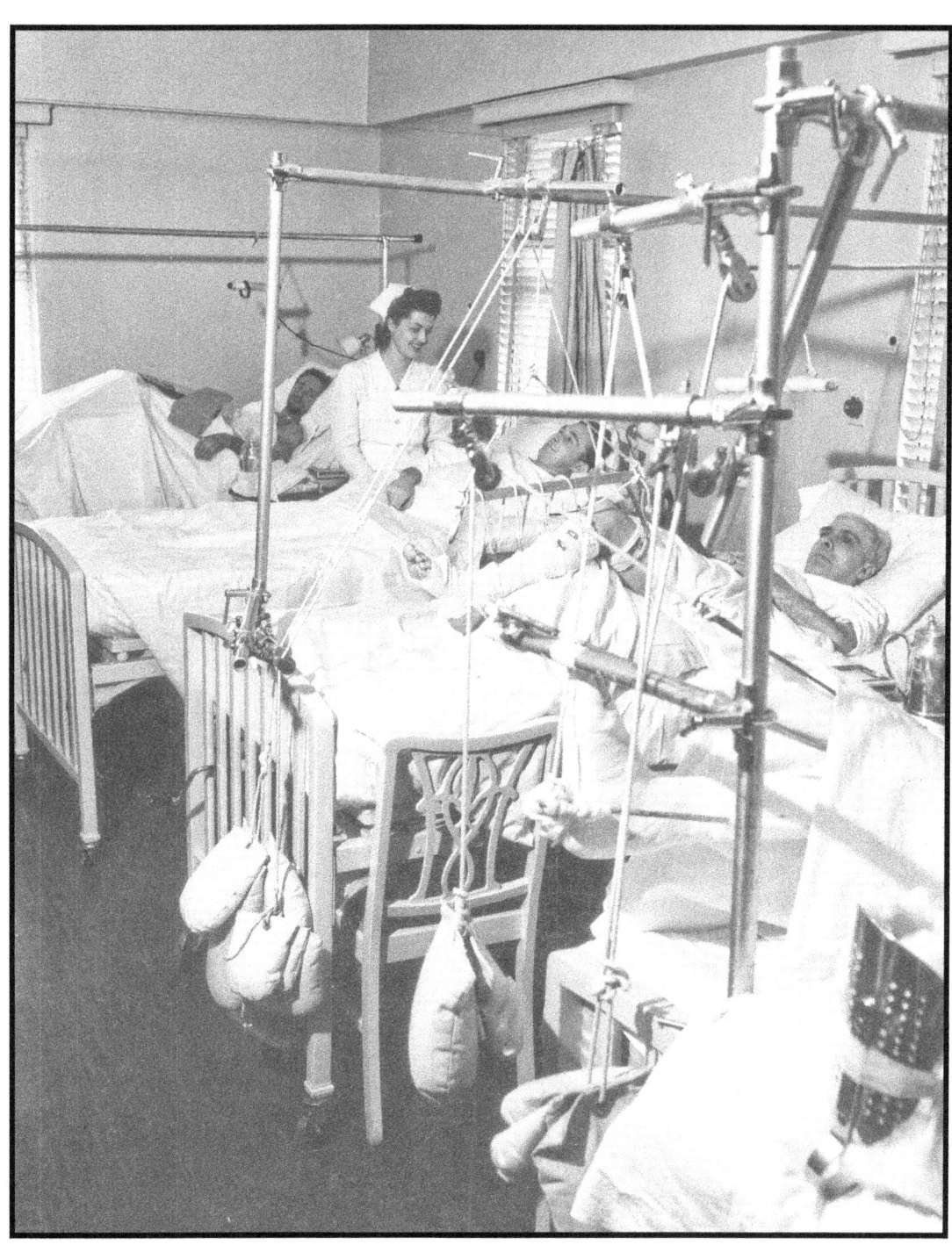

Men's ward showing patients in traction beds, Fabiola Hospital, Oakland.

Previous Pages: HJK and BFK in front of Permanente Foundation plaque.
The Permanente Foundation, a nonprofit organization, was formed in July 1942 to operate the Richmond Field Hospital and the Fabiola Hospital in Oakland that provided inpatient services for workers injured on the job as well as for those enrolled in the Permanente Health Plan.

A Special Kaiser Permanente *Anniversary*

I wrote this review of the history of the Kaiser Permanente Health Plan in 2007 for the sixty-fifth anniversary of the founding of the Permanente Health Plan, the organization that would later become the Kaiser Permanente Health Plan. This article and those that follow examine and celebrate the wartime shipyard years that shaped the early development of "the most important social institution to come out of World War II." It is a tribute to that institution that at an age when retirement looms large in most people's lives, Kaiser Permanente seems to have discovered rejuvenation in a number of forms including the application of computers to health care delivery, evidence-based medicine, and innovative hospital construction and design.

On March 3, 2007, Kaiser Permanente reached the sixty-fifth anniversary of its humble beginnings as an industrial health program filling the medical needs of the workers in Henry Kaiser's amazingly successful World War II shipyards. On March 3, 1942, the physician-founder of what would develop into Kaiser Permanente opened his first medical office to take care of the thousands of workers Henry Kaiser was hiring in Richmond, California. At this time, the predecessor to the Permanente Medical Group* consisted only of Drs. Sidney Garfield and his friend and colleague, Cecil

---

*Originally all the physicians, including Dr. Cutting, were employees of Sidney Garfield and Associates. However, in 1948, Garfield turned over ownership of the practice to the participating physicians, believing it was better for them to work for themselves than for someone else. The physicians selected the name it still holds, the Permanente Medical Group. It has been estimated that at the time the practice was worth $1,000,000. His gift is an example of generosity, unique in American medicine.

Cutting, who had worked with Garfield at the Grand Coulee Dam construction site in Washington State.

The first medical office for the brand-new program was in Oakland on what was then and is still known as "Pill Hill" (because of the cluster of hospitals and medical offices located on the small hill). In those first days, Dr. Cutting saw shipyard patients in the afternoons in the new office after spending the morning performing surgery at nearby Merritt Hospital, which owned the burned-out shell that had been Fabiola Hospital. Part of the deal Garfield made when he purchased the abandoned hospital was that he and his staff could have access to up to twenty Merritt beds while the old hospital was being renovated. That way he could be sure to have a place to hospitalize the new program's patients.

The largest private health care program in the United States began on a shoestring. Years later, Dr. Cutting remembered that one particularly unusual feature of his new office was a one-way mirror that allowed him to look out directly from his office into the lobby, making it possible for him to run the office without a receptionist, at least until someone could be hired.

Garfield quickly discovered he needed more beds than the twenty at Merritt Hospital, and before long, Cutting and the new physicians joining Sidney Garfield and Associates were also placing patients in county hospitals and at Stanford University's Lane Hospital in San Francisco. These were temporary expedients until Fabiola, also called Permanente Hospital, was ready. Renovation, equipping, and staffing of the new hospital were completed in the short time of only five months.

Even at this early stage, Dr. Garfield was aware that opposition to his prepaid group practice medical care program was beginning to bubble to the surface. Area physicians were becoming worried about the competition and what it might cost them. Garfield decided to try to reduce their economic concerns by agreeing to limit his wartime prepayment work to industrial care only. What was then called the Permanente Health Plan (sometimes simply referred to as the Plan) was open at first only to shipyard workers. Later in the war it became possible for their families to join. Only at war's end was it opened to the public. Today Kaiser Permanente uses that 1945 date, when the Plan was opened to the public, to mark the beginning of the program, but Dr. Garfield always thought of 1942 in the shipyards as the true beginning.

Dr. Garfield and Dr. Kay Have Dinner at the Presidio*

Two physicians, Sidney Garfield, recently released from the U.S. Army after one of the shortest careers in military history, and Lt. Raymond Kay, a reservist who had just been called up to active duty, met for dinner in San Francisco at the army post known as the Presidio. The United States had entered World War II a few months earlier, and Dr. Kay was on temporary assignment to the Army's Letterman Hospital, waiting to be shipped out to India with his unit. Neither man had any idea that their

Sidney R. Garfield, M.D. at podium during dedication of Fabiola Hospital, August 1942.

Although disappointed at having to go into the army without his friend, Sidney, Dr. Ray Kay rose through the officer ranks of the U.S. Army Medical Corps to the rank of Lieutenant Colonel.

*Much of the material for this article is drawn from the oral history resources of Kaiser Permanente's archives.

quiet dinner would be a landmark in the development of a model for the rational organization of health care for future generations and into the next century. What they were doing that evening, though, was creating the foundation of what would develop into the largest nonprofit health care delivery system in the nation.

Raymond Kay and Sidney Garfield had been close personal and professional friends going back to when Dr. Kay had begun his internship at Los Angeles County Hospital ten years before. Dr. Garfield had been the hospital's chief surgical resident at the time. Along with a third physician, Ray Kay's roommate J. Wallace "Wally" Neighbor, who would also play a major role in the development of Kaiser Permanente, the young doctors worked together, played tennis and ping-pong, and when they had some free time, they double-dated. They also spent long hours learning from each other. Dr. Kay later recalled this period of his life:

> *When he [Dr. Garfield] was on duty at night as a surgical resident, seeing all of the acute abdomens and other acute cases, I would very frequently join him, and I learned a tremendous amount. Likewise, he would spend a lot of time with me in my medical wards and we would learn from each other. And we felt that one of the wonderful things about our training was that we learned from each other, that we shared our patients and shared our knowledge, and we learned a great deal. And we thought, "Wouldn't it be wonderful if we could practice medicine that way and have the fellowship and that learning develop from each other?"*

The two physicians realized that there was something else about this kind of hospital practice that worked out very well for both doctor and patient. Dr. Kay described it:

> *… we were very impressed with the fact that there were no economic blocks. Whatever the patients needed, we could do for them. Whatever we needed—the lab work, the x-rays, to diagnose them or to treat them—we*

were able to do, and there was nothing that stopped us. That seemed to be wonderful. Then we started thinking, "Wouldn't it be wonderful if we could really practice as a doctor with a group of doctors where you could share knowledge and share experience and share patients, and where you could take care of people with no economic blocks?"

Looking back forty-five years later, Dr. Kay added proudly, "I guess we were dreaming, even then."

In late 1933, Sidney Garfield had left L.A. County to open his own little hospital in the Mojave Desert to take care of the sick and injured men building the Colorado River Aqueduct. Dr. Kay had been a frequent visitor. Of course, Garfield had invited his friend to join his staff, but Kay had preferred to stay at L.A. County. There he was continually presented with a far wider variety of cases than he would ever see in an industrial medicine practice. Although he wished Dr. Garfield the best of luck, Kay had felt it would not be good for his professional development to go out to the desert with his friend.

Dr. Garfield's tiny, temporary 12-bed hospital in the Mojave Desert was the beginning of today's Kaiser Permanente.

Kay had watched with concern as Garfield's desert hospital had sunk into debt. Then he saw how switching from fee-for-service to prepayment* had transformed the economics of medicine. The little hospital had prospered, at the same time giving better care for the sick and injured workers. It had also provided greater professional satisfaction for the physicians who had been loosened from the oversight of insurance companies and now had greater freedom to exercise their professional judgment. Both

---

* In fee-for-service, medical services are provided and paid for individually. The patient, or his insurance company, pays separately for each service and procedure. In prepaid group practice, the patient agrees that for a monthly fee, he will be able to receive medical care, as needed, from the group of physicians with whom he has contracted.

Mason City Hospital, Grand Coulee Dam.

men dreamed of someday having the opportunity to try out their developing theories on a larger scale.

In 1938, Garfield was offered that chance. At the request of Henry Kaiser, he had been able to set up a prepaid program to take care of the 5,000 workers building the Grand Coulee Dam.* It was a challenge, but Garfield soon had the local hospital remodeled to his specifications and had assembled a very capable medical staff. It was clear that the program was working. Soon the workers' families were clamoring to be accepted into the plan. The construction workers were so pleased with the care they were getting that they threatened to go out on strike if their families could not be included in their coverage. The Kaisers were pleased, the construction workers were pleased, and the doctors found that the economic freedom under prepayment made possible a great deal of professional satisfaction that they felt would not be available in private practice.

However, Garfield still thought of himself primarily as a surgeon. When the chief of surgery at University of Southern California Medical School, Clarence Berne, offered him a position as a surgical "super resident" (known at other hospitals as senior resident) back at L.A. County Hospital, Garfield had accepted enthusiastically. He felt it was a better way to expand and sharpen his surgical skills than practicing in remote eastern Washington State. He left the Coulee program in the hands of Wally Neighbor and Cecil Cutting, a Stanford-trained surgeon whom he had recruited from San Francisco County Hospital.

---

* Grand Coulee Dam, on the Columbia River, is one of the largest dams in the world and the world's largest concrete structure. The idea of damming the Columbia River at Grand Coulee was considered by many to be impossible. A construction consortium led by Henry Kaiser finished the project ahead of schedule and under budget.

Back at L.A. County Hospital, once again, Garfield and Kay spent hours talking about not just their challenging cases but also about the larger issue of the inequities of contemporary health care. Ray Kay was particularly bothered by the fact that while they were providing excellent care at teaching centers such as L.A. County, ". . . our good residents and doctors go to waste on Wilshire Boulevard. They would go down there where they weren't needed and pretty soon at the lunch table, instead of talking about interesting cases, they were talking about the stock market and how much it cost to take care of people." Garfield and Kay wondered, "What can we do to get people to go into the country instead of Wilshire Boulevard, so you get the proper distribution?"

Ray Kay, a self-described "spoiled brat" as a youth, had been sent to military schools for his high school education and had come to enjoy the discipline and the camaraderie. Perhaps that was one of the reasons why, as war clouds gathered in Europe, he had accepted a commission as a lieutenant in the U.S. Army Reserves. Several months before, he had been called up to active duty and had been later assigned to a unit forming from the staff of the L.A. County Hospital. He was now stationed at Letterman Hospital at the Presidio in San Francisco and scheduled to ship out in a matter of days.

Immediately following Pearl Harbor, Garfield had volunteered for Army service and had joined the same unit, also with the rank of lieutenant. However, while the two men were awaiting orders to ship out to India with their unit, Garfield had again accepted a request from Henry Kaiser and his sons, Henry, Jr. and Edgar. This time it was to design a medical program for their rapidly expanding shipyard work force. Henry Kaiser had decided that the only person who could really set up and operate such a complex program was Lieutenant Sidney Garfield, M.D. Without telling Garfield, the industrialist had sent his most trusted aide, A.B. Ordway, to Washington,

D.C. to get the physician released from the military. "Ord" was soon back in Oakland with an order signed by President Roosevelt. After what may have been one of the shortest military careers on record, Dr. Garfield was free to perform a vital civilian service.

When he heard about the change in Garfield's plans, Dr. Kay was upset. He had been looking forward to sharing his Army adventure with his friend. Now the two men, the civilian Garfield and the Lieutenant Kay, were meeting for what was to be the last time before Dr. Kay sailed for India. Garfield later described that meeting: "Ray was mad as hell. 'You told me you were going into the army. I wanted to go in with you!'"

Garfield tried to get his friend to understand that the Kaiser shipyards offered an unusual opportunity to put the principles they had been discussing for so many years into large-scale operation. Kay finally agreed. "I'll forgive you on two conditions. One, you set this thing up so it's a foundation that you don't own, like you did on the desert and at Coulee. Set it up as a foundation, because then we can use it for funds for research, and stuff like that. The other thing is that you don't pay your doctors any more than the Army doctors get paid." There was a third condition, too. Garfield promised Kay that after the war "we'll start a health plan in Los Angeles." Garfield added, "I wanted to do that too, because that was my home, you know, and we grew up at the County Hospital."

By the end of dinner that night, Garfield and Kay had agreed on some of the basic ideas that would shape the Permanente Health Plan. Wartime "profits" from the operation of the health plan would be set aside for later use, and after the war, the program would expand into Southern California. Most importantly for the future, the program would become nonprofit, with major implications for Kaiser Permanente.

Prelude to the Permanente Health Plan

Before Drs. Garfield and Kay met for dinner at the Presidio, Garfield had already attempted to set up a prepaid health plan at the new shipyards in Richmond. By June 1941 Kaiser's work force at the Richmond yards had already doubled to 30,000. Unemployed workers from all over America streamed into Richmond, eager for their first steady work since the beginning of the Depression. Despite vigorous training and safety programs, with so many inexperienced workers entering ship construction, it was inevitable that there would be a great many injuries. Since at this time only nine percent of Americans had hospital insurance and only two percent were covered for medical services, it would be necessary to provide some kind of medical care for them. According to John Smillie in his book *The Story of the Permanente Medical Group*, a local physician, Dr. L. Paul Fraser, was the only doctor available in Richmond.

With more workers being hired every day, it was obvious that one physician could not hope to handle all their medical needs. Even the thirty or so doctors who were practicing in nearby towns were soon overwhelmed by the new shipyard workers and their families. Access to medical care was becoming a serious problem. In one heartbreaking case, a child died as her mother carried her from one crowded physician's waiting room to another, trying to find someone who had time to see her little girl. By the time she found one, 50 miles away, in Palo Alto, it was too late.

Workers who had been with Kaiser up at the Grand Coulee Dam and had followed him to Richmond started to grumble and ask why they could not have as good care in Richmond as they had had at the dam. Morale, and therefore productivity, was threatened, and, as the yards grew and more men were hired, it was clear that things would only get worse.

A False Start

HJK's younger son, Henry Kaiser, Jr. decided to tackle the shipyard medical problem. With the approval of Clay Bedford, general manager of the shipyards, he turned to Sidney Garfield for help. The younger Kaiser asked him to come up from Los Angeles to design a system based on the same principles that had worked so well at the big dam.

One of Dr. Garfield's initial concerns was hostility from the local medical societies if he were to come into the East Bay with a new healthcare delivery system. He was well aware that the only reason that organized medicine had not attacked the program at Grand Coulee was that it had been so remote. There had been hardly any other doctors for miles around. Right at the start Garfield and HJK, Jr. surveyed local physicians. When they discovered they would actually welcome help, Garfield started planning.

Working intensely for two weeks, Dr. Garfield drew up a detailed prospectus based on a field hospital, medical offices, and first aid stations, to be operated by a prepaid medical group. Along with Clay Bedford and Henry Kaiser, Jr., he presented his plan to the shipyards' insurance underwriters. These companies were key to any program design because as underwriters of the Workmen's Compensation Program, they would have to agree to participate in the prepayment element. However, these companies had no experience with prepayment and were unwilling to commit themselves to supporting any plan in which it was the cornerstone. To the great disappointment of Garfield, as well as Bedford and HJK, Jr. the insurance companies turned it down. Garfield returned to his teaching position at the Los Angeles County Hospital. The young Kaiser and Clay Bedford were left to figure out how to solve a problem which was getting worse by the day. What no one could foresee was that the attack on Pearl Harbor would change everything, even health care.

Shortly after December 7, 1941, Henry Kaiser, Jr. asked Garfield to come back up to the shipyards. He wanted to make another try at selling their plan to the insurance companies, whom he felt, correctly as it turned out, would be more open to innovation in this national emergency. In the meantime, Dr. Garfield had enlisted in the U.S. Army Medical Corps and had received a commission as a first lieutenant. He was scheduled to ship out overseas with his unit in a few weeks. Even so, he agreed to see what he could do to help, and arrived at the Kaiser offices in military uniform for what he thought would be a temporary consulting job. As HJK, Jr. and Clay Bedford had hoped, given the new circumstances, the insurance companies fell into line and agreed to support the Garfield plan.

Henry Kaiser was convinced that the best person to run what was looking more and more like a key part of shipyard operations was Dr. Garfield. The Kaisers convinced Garfield to come up once again and work out the remaining details of the program.

Fabiola Hospital, Oakland, on opening day, August 1942.

The Permanente Health Plan
Begins Operation

In early March 1942, three months after the attack on Pearl Harbor, Sidney Garfield was struggling to get his new health care program into operation. As yet, he had no facilities he could call his own and almost no staff. Despite the size and complexity of the task ahead, the thirty-five-year-old doctor was confident that he could get a successful program underway. In a 1974 television interview, stored in the archives of Kaiser Permanente, Dr. Garfield recalled those days:

> *We actually had very little concern about the size of the job. Our big concern was to get the personnel, facilities and the equipment to do the job. . . . We were looking for a place to get started. I looked around Oakland for where we could get hospital facilities, and saw this shell of a structure standing on Broadway and MacArthur. It had been a part of the old Fabiola Hospital, which had burned down, but this . . . part was built of concrete and hadn't burned down. . . . It had been given to Merritt Hospital, so I approached Dr. Black, who was the head of Merritt Hospital, and asked him if he would sell.*

The rundown hospital building was useless in the condition it was in at the time. Dr. Black, the head of Merritt Hospital, had been willing to part with the building, but the price was high, and having the shell of an abandoned hospital would solve only one part of Garfield's problem. It would be several months before the damaged building could be transformed into a working hospital. Dr. Garfield insisted that a part of his agreement to buy the old hospital had to be a guarantee of beds at Merritt Hospital for his patients until his new hospital was ready.

Garfield offered to buy the hospital at Merritt's asking price of $50,000. "I'll buy it if you'll let us use twenty beds in your hospital, for industrial accidents, until I fix it up." Now assured that he had at least twenty beds for injured and ill shipyard workers, he continued discussions with other hospitals in the East Bay and in San Francisco to find the additional beds he would need until the Permanente Fabiola building was ready.

Garfield was careful to include the specific words, "industrial accidents" in his discussions with Dr. Black at Merritt and with administrators and physicians of other local hospitals. Despite the wartime crisis, East Bay physicians were more than a little concerned about the economic consequences of a whole group of doctors moving into what had formerly been their "territory." Garfield's voluntary restriction of his practice to industrial work, at least in the beginning, reassured the established physicians and probably made it a bit easier for Garfield to get hospital beds during the transition.

The search for the money to buy and renovate the old Fabiola Hospital went through a number of stages. The first company to approach Dr. Garfield with an offer was Industrial Indemnity. Not coincidentally, this was the same insurance company that had led the change from fee-for-service to prepayment for Dr. Garfield eight years before. By doing so, the company had saved Sidney Garfield's first hospital, which was taking care of workers building the aqueduct that would bring Colorado River water to Los Angeles. There the economics based on the traditional fee-for-service model had not worked out, and Garfield was facing bankruptcy. It had been insurance executive Harold Hatch, a vice president of the Industrial Indemnity Company, who had proposed what would become years later the basic element of Kaiser Permanente.

He had offered that instead of paying Garfield for each treatment for each patient, his company would prepay a nickel a day for each worker covered under his plan, providing the only income for the hospital. This simple change, soon adopted by the other insurance companies covering aqueduct workers, had saved the hospital. It had also turned medical economics upside-down by supplying a financial incentive for preventive care. The experiment had worked out well for everyone and had led, in a roundabout way, to Garfield and Kaiser teaming up at the shipyards.

Industrial Indemnity had seen how well the system worked, both for the company, for the construction contractors, and for the sick and injured. They were now willing to do the same for him in Richmond and Oakland; they would advance him the money to build the facilities he needed. In his 1974 interview, Garfield recalled that "I had an offer from the Industrial Indemnity Exchange, that they would loan me $500,000 to start the operation." However, an objection to this plan came from a surprising source. Henry Kaiser convinced Garfield that he would be better off going to a third party for the money he needed rather than dealing with an insurance company he would be serving. Kaiser explained that it would give Garfield more independence to have an outside funding source. "I said, 'Fine. Where do we start?' He said, 'Well, let's go see Giannini.'"

"Giannini" was Amadeo Peter, "A.P." Giannini, the founder and president of the Bank of America and a legend in the financial community. At the time of the great San Francisco Earthquake in 1906, Giannini's first bank, the Bank of Italy, had been in operation for not quite two years. As fires swept across the city, with several of his most trusted employees, he had carried his bank assets, through streets blocked with rubble and fire engines racing to try to contain the flames, to safety at his San Mateo home. The next day at a meeting of the city's bankers, the general feeling was that it would be six months before the city's financial institutions would be able to recover from the inevitable chaos that included the loss of many of their records. The bankers argued that it would be weeks before their vaults would have cooled enough to open. Young Giannini—age thirty-five—stood up on a chair and said:

> *Gentlemen, to follow the course you are suggesting will be a vital mistake. If you keep your banks closed until November, you might as well keep them closed. In November there will be no city or people left to serve. Today is the time they need you. The time for doing business is right now. Tomorrow morning, I am putting a desk on Washington Street wharf with a Bank of Italy sign over it. Any man who wants to rebuild San Francisco can come there and get as much cash as he needs to do it. I advise all you bankers to beg, borrow or steal a desk and follow my example."* [Julian Dana, *A.P. Giannini: Giant of the West* (New York: Prentice-Hall, 1947)]

The financial institution Giannini had founded at the turn of the twentieth century in a San Francisco storefront had survived the earthquake and prospered during the rebuilding of that city, making loans that helped to restore San Francisco to economic health. Giannini had introduced the idea of branch banking, and, by investing the money of tens of thousands of small depositors rather than restricting himself to big business accounts, which was the custom of the day, he turned his small, local bank into a national financial institution, the Bank of America. It became the source of much of the capital used to develop industry in the American West. Kaiser relied heavily on Giannini and the Bank of America for financing his projects, and the relationship had benefited both men.

Giannini had both imagination and vision. A few years earlier, he had sat attentively through a presentation by a thirty-four-year-old cartoonist who recited and sang selections from a movie script of a kind no one had yet created—a full-length animation feature. Cartoons were believed to work well as funny, short subjects, but not considered suitable for longer narrative productions The cartoonist needed money to carry out his project. Giannini had been impressed enough to extend a one-million-dollar line of credit to Walt Disney. The classic film *Snow White* was the result.

As much of a visionary as he was, when Garfield approached him for a loan to renovate the Fabiola Hospital for the shipyard workers, Giannini turned him down. According to him, lending money to build a hospital was not good business.

Three decades later, Dr. Garfield recalled, "He laughed at us. 'We won't loan a penny to hospitals. They never—never—can pay off, and if you try to foreclose on them, what do you do with a hospital?'" The banker did offer an alternative, though. "Henry, if you want to guarantee the loan, I'll let you have $250,000." Kaiser agreed. Garfield had the money he needed: $50,000 for purchasing the hospital and $200,000 for remodeling.

While Dr. Garfield was working on acquiring a hospital, he was also recruiting physicians—by phone, letter, and personal visits. The first to sign on was his friend Cecil Cutting who had been with him at Grand Coulee Dam.

With construction at the dam slowing down, Dr. Cutting had left Garfield's group to take a position at Virginia Mason Hospital, a multi-specialty group practice in Seattle that operated by many of the same principles he had seen work so well at Grand Coulee. Dr. Garfield convinced his friend to come down to Oakland for a visit so he could show him the facilities that would be the framework for an industry-based, prepaid, group specialty practice to care for the shipyard workers.

Half a century later, Dr. Cutting laughed when he thought back on that first visit to the abandoned hulk that had been the Fabiola Hospital. The building had been abandoned for several years and many of the inside walls had been knocked down.

Dr. Cutting, along with Henry Kaiser and Sidney Garfield, had to pick his way down crumbling staircases and across floors covered with rubble. Twisted pipes, no longer connected at either end, lay around them in senseless convolutions. "It was a long way from being a hospital," he remembered. Dr. Garfield was very apologetic about the condition of the hospital, but HJK had interrupted him, "What's the matter, young man, don't you think I have any imagination?" Kaiser's optimism was infectious. When Sidney Garfield offered Dr. Cutting the joint position of chief of staff and chief of surgery at both the Permanente Fabiola Hospital and the Richmond Field Hospital, he immediately accepted.

On March 1, 1942, Dr. Cutting officially joined the Permanente Health Plan as its first physician. Dr. Cutting and his wife Millie, a registered nurse, left Seattle for California. Things were moving too fast for the Cuttings to have found a home yet, so Sidney put them up temporarily in the fashionable Claremont Hotel in Berkeley until they could find a place of their own. Cutting remembered that the luxury of the Claremont bore no relation to the gritty reality of getting the new medical care program underway.

The Richmond Field Hospital not quite ready for business.

On Dr. Cutting's first day, March 3, 1942, Dr. Garfield showed him what would soon be the Richmond Field Hospital. Construction crews were still digging the foundation out of a small sea of mud. The first goal was to get enough of the hospital up so that they could begin operation in what Dr. Cutting called "a glorified first aid station."

Expansion was to continue throughout the war. The little box-like structure in the middle of the mud would soon be transformed into a 185-bed hospital. Meanwhile, in Oakland, the hospital that would be known as Permanente Fabiola was being renovated as rapidly as possible to become the cornerstone of the new health care program.

Although an orthopedist named Gerry Gill helped out with patients for a few months, Dr. Cutting was mostly on his own until Garfield managed to recruit additional physicians. In the mornings, Dr. Cutting operated at Merritt Hospital, and in the afternoons, he saw patients at the office on "Pill Hill." Dr. Cutting even made time to make house calls. Both he and Garfield were also working to figure out the designs and supplies needed for the Richmond and Oakland facilities. With hardly anyone paying attention, what would develop into the world's largest nongovernmental, prepaid, group specialty, integrated practice had begun operation on a side street in Oakland.

By the time the Richmond Field Hospital and the Permanente Fabiola Hospital went into operation a few months later, in August 1942, Garfield had managed to recruit a sizeable and well-qualified medical staff. Many who joined at this time would remain with Dr. Garfield in the postwar years as pioneers of the Kaiser Permanente program.

Postscript: Establishing a medical care program for the Richmond shipyards despite the special challenges of wartime material shortages and the wholesale draft of physicians into the military was an impressive demonstration of Garfield's abilities as a physician-leader. Simultaneously he took over the responsibility of meeting the medical needs of the workers at the rapidly growing Kaiser shipyards at Vancouver-Portland for a total of more than 200,000 members.

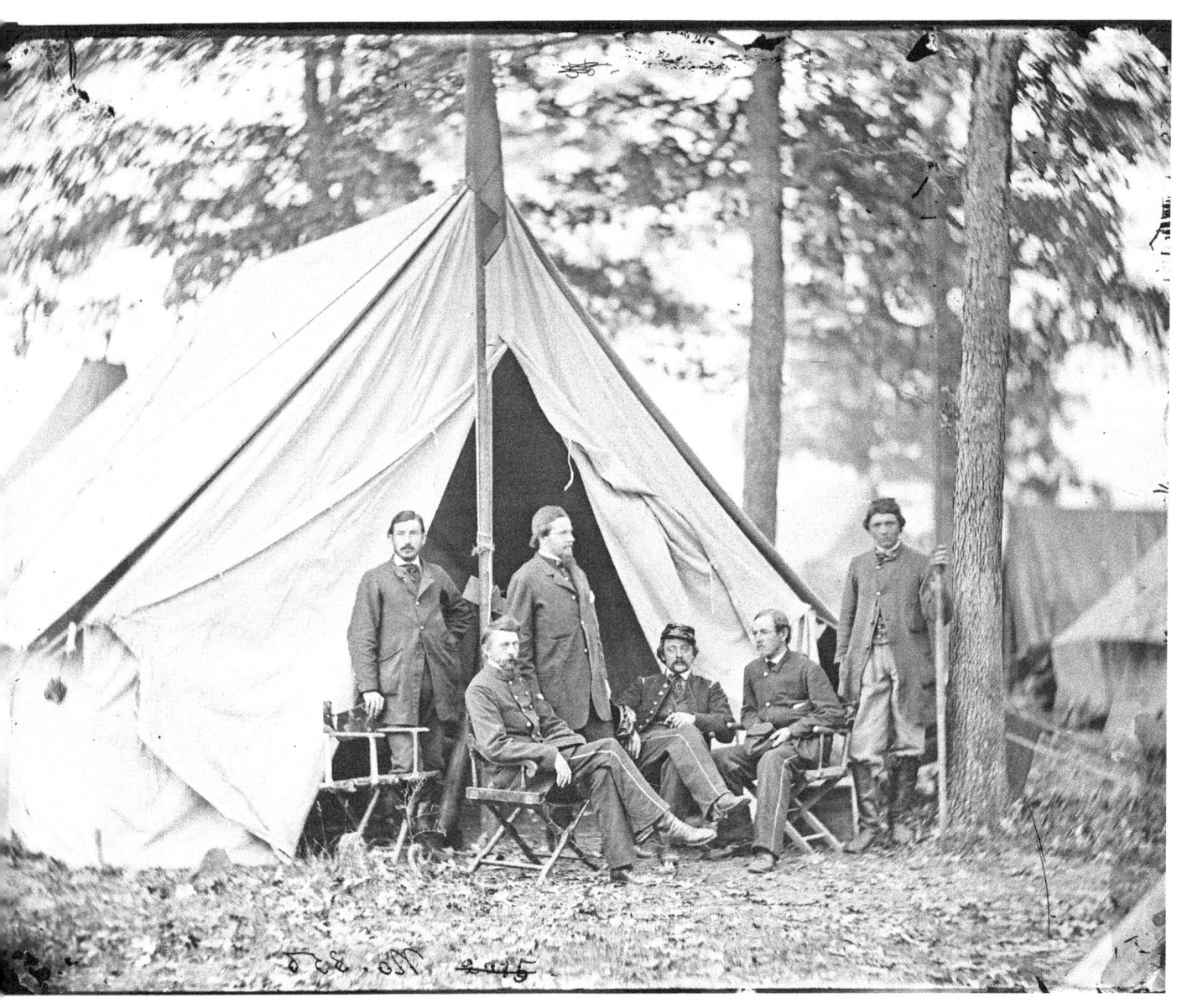
Major Jonathan Letterman (seated left) and his staff, Warrenton, Virginia, 1862.

Organizing Care in the *Richmond Shipyards*

The model that Sidney Garfield had selected for his medical care program was a well-tested one. It had been developed eighty years earlier by Dr. Jonathan Letterman during the Civil War. Letterman's model had proven so successful that a grateful U.S. Army had named the hospital in the San Francisco Presidio for the physician who had developed it. Coincidentally, this was the hospital where Dr. Raymond Kay had been temporarily assigned, making it possible for the two friends to meet for that landmark dinner in San Francisco.

The importance of Letterman's contribution grew from the fact that both Union and Confederate military leaders had been caught by surprise by the massive casualties that had resulted from the increased effectiveness of their modernized weapons. When the war began, the Army Medical Department, responsible for the care of the sick and wounded, had a staff of only ninety doctors. These physicians, accustomed to dealing with the health problems of small military outposts, had no idea of how to deal with the large-scale medical and logistical problems of the giant citizen armies being fielded in this war. Armies consisting of 100,000 to 150,000 men were going into battle, and the casualties were often running at a horrific one soldier in five, sometimes one in four, and even, as would later happen at the Battle of Gettysburg, one in three. After the second battle at Bull Run, it took a week to collect all the wounded from the battlefield. Not only was this a humanitarian disaster, but the generals realized it was affecting morale and the effectiveness of their troops. Dr. Letterman took on the job of trying to figure out the best way to organize medical care and he came up with a three-tiered system which is still in use by the military today.

A comparison of Dr. Letterman's and Dr. Garfield's systems demonstrate a clear resemblance between the two.

The First Aid Station

First aid station in Shipyard No. 3. The first aid building in Yard Three is the only one to have survived to the present. It is an example of the art deco style that was a feature of the major permanent structures of Yard Three.

Letterman Plan: A "Battalion Field Aid Station" would be set up directly behind the front lines. According to Letterman, "The chief functions of an Aid Station were to stop bleeding, relieve pain, reduce fractures and dislocations, and stabilize the wounded for evacuation to the Field Hospital." Medical orderlies would bring the wounded who were unable to walk to the Field Aid Station by ambulance.

Garfield Plan: Injured shipyard workers would go to the first aid station located inside each shipyard. A fleet of ambulances was available for transportation if needed. Physicians and nurses were on duty at each first aid station and specially trained workers, "First Aid Men," were scattered about the yards in the busiest working areas, such as the prefabrication shops and the shipways.

The Field Hospital

Letterman Plan: Field Hospitals were established three to five miles behind the lines, safe from any artillery fire. They were staffed by surgeons, assistant surgeons, additional hospital stewards, and other assigned male personnel. The chief function of the field hospital was to perform emergency surgery and to prepare the wounded for further evacuation.

Shipyard ambulances and their "First Aid Men" drivers carrying their black bags stand ready outside of shipyard first aid.

Garfield Plan: With no danger of artillery fire, the Richmond Field Hospital could be located closer to the shipyards than it would have been under the Letterman plan, but during the early years of the war, it served roughly the same purpose. The seriously injured were stabilized there before being sent to the Permanente Fabiola Hospital in Oakland for further treatment. Most patients were transported in less than forty-eight hours. The hospital also acted as a clinic. In fact, because of the importance of providing workers easy access to medical care as

Richmond Field Hospital with wartime additions.

soon as possible, the Field Hospital first opened as a clinic, without any hospital beds. Construction of the first hospital wing, with ten beds, began immediately after the clinic was ready. By March 1943, the capacity of the Richmond Field Hospital had been increased to about seventy-five beds.

The Large Hospital

Letterman's plan called for a large hospital to which the wounded would be transferred after stabilization. However, since so many of the amputations and body wounds were ultimately fatal due to infections, only a small percentage of the seriously wounded made it there.

Garfield Plan: The large hospital was actually the centerpiece of the new program. Here all elective surgery was done and patients recovered from injuries and illness. At that time, hospitalization was a major part of the program. For example, according to Dr. John Smillie, himself a program pioneer and early historian of the Permanente Medical Group, appendectomy patients were kept in the hospital for seven to ten days; hernia repairs for about two weeks.

In the Civil War illness had been a greater killer than artillery, bullets, and bayonets. For every soldier killed in battle, two died of diseases, particularly dysentery, diarrhea, typhoid, and malaria. Soldiers from isolated rural areas suffered from childhood diseases such as measles and mumps because they lacked immunity of those who had grown up in the more crowded cities.

While Garfield's staff saw a great many of the industrial equivalents of battle wounds, particularly burns and fractures (13,000 in the first two years), there was plenty of illness as well. In a workforce made up mostly of men too old or too sick for military duty, pneumonia was the major disease. Permanente physicians were seeing literally thousands of such cases. By analyzing what approaches worked best, doctors were able to reduce mortality statistics significantly below those anywhere else in the nation. Garfield's physicians were pleased and proud when Dr. William Kerr, chairman of the Department of Medicine at the University of California San Francisco Medical School, arranged for UCSF interns to rotate through Permanente for the experience. They saw this as an independent confirmation of what they already believed: that in those very difficult times they were providing high-quality medical care.

The organized care provided under the Letterman plan during the Civil War also brought about important improvements in clinical care. Army medical officers came to understand that strict sanitary standards could reduce the spread of disease. Their experience with thousands of postoperative infections, such as hospital gangrene, led to successful research in ways to prevent it, saving many lives in the decades that followed. Doctors treated hundreds of thousands of cases of dysentery, diarrhea, typhoid, malaria, and gunshot wounds, and they compiled voluminous notes that were the subjects of valuable studies published after the war.

Permanente physicians also saw tuberculosis, polio, typhoid fever, pneumococcal, streptococcal, and staphylococcal infections, and even a half-dozen cases of leprosy. Surgeon Norman Haugen, who joined the program during World War II, remembers that during the 1920s and 1930s, when hernias had been repaired with absorbable sutures, the recurrence rate had been very high. He recalls that even though it was "an existing condition," and technically not the responsibility of the health plan to treat, it was so important to get workers back on the job that hernia repair was one of the most common surgical procedures performed on shipyard workers.

PERMANENTE FOUNDATION HOSPITALS

OAKLAND — RICHMOND

SIDNEY R. GARFIELD, M.D., & ASSOCIATES
C.C. CUTTING, M.D., CHIEF OF STAFF
RICHARD MOORE, M.D., ASST. CHIEF OF STAFF

DERMATOLOGY
- BROOKS PRINGLE, M.D., DIRECTOR
- GEORGE B. ANDERSON, M.D.

EAR NOSE & THROAT
- I. H. WIESENFELD, M.D., DIRECTOR
- JAMES H. MC CLELLAND, M.D.
- LENA ENGST THIRIOT, M.D.
- BENJAMIN THOMAS, M.D.

EYE
- THOMAS G. SCHNOOR, M.D., DIRECTOR
- F. B. MC DONALD, M.D.
- ARTHUR LAYTON, D. OPT.

INTERNAL MEDICINE
- MORRIS F. COLLEN, M.D., DIRECTOR
- EUGENE B. LEVINE, M.D., ASST. DIRECTOR
- DONALD W. ASH, M.D.
- FREDERICK BURT, M.D.
- THURMAN DANNENBERG, M.D.
- J. F. DIDDLE, M.D.
- FRANZ R. GOETZL, M.D.
- ERIC C. KAST, M.D.
- GEORGE O'BRIEN, M.D.
- EDWARD PHILLIPS, M.D.
- PHILLIP J. RAIMONDI, M.D.
- WILLIAM RICE, M.D.
- ALVIN L. SELLERS, M.D.
- MARGARET STUART, M.D.
- ALEXANDER WITKOW, M.D.

NEUROLOGY
- J. P. FITZGIBBON, M.D., DIRECTOR

OBSTETRICS & GYNECOLOGY
- WILSON FOOTER, M.D., DIRECTOR
- LAWRENCE ALLRED, M.D.
- HANNAH PETERS, M.D.
- MARY H. REHM, M.D.
- ELSE ROSS, M.D.
- O. D. WILLIAMS, M.D.

ORTHOPEDICS
- C. C. CUTTING, M.D., DIRECTOR
- PETER J. BARONE, M.D.
- JOHN P. EVANS, M.D.
- LLOYD D. FISHER, M.D.
- THOS. FLINT, JR., M.D.
- E. E. FRANKLIN, M.D.
- A. BERNARD GRAY, M.D.
- WILLIAM HATTEROTH, M.D.
- N. MEADOFF, M.D.
- RICHARD MOORE, M.D.
- H. C. PEDERSON, M.D.

PATHOLOGY
- STANLEY L. REA, M.D., DIRECTOR

PEDIATRICS
- ALEXANDER HATOFF, M.D., DIRECTOR
- DAVID BRUSER, M.D.
- MOLLIE CHOLFIN, M.D.
- POOI TUEN (BEATRICE) LEI, M.D.
- DELPHINE PALM, M.D.

PUBLIC HEALTH
- CLIFFORD KUH, M.D., DIRECTOR

RADIOLOGY
- OTTO HATSCHEK, M.D., DIRECTOR

SURGERY
- R. BRUCE HENLEY, M.D., DIRECTOR
- A. LA MONT BARITELL, M.D.
- JAMES A. BASYE, M.D.
- JOHN BLEMER, M.D.
- DAVID G. BORDEN, M.D.
- WILLIAM F. BOYER, M.D.
- H. DONALD GRANT, M.D.
- NORMAN L. HAUGEN, M.D.
- ROBERT A. MENDLE, M.D.
- DON C. MUSSER, M.D.
- LEO D. NANNINI, M.D.

UROLOGY
- MILTON Z. LONDON, M.D., DIRECTOR
- C. LESLIE COLLINS, M.D.

GENERAL
- WILLIAMS BARNES, M.D.
- ISABELLA CLINTON, M.D.
- DARRELL HAWLEY, M.D.
- DAVID HIBBS, M.D.
- SAMUEL JAFFEE, M.D.
- ROBERT JONES, M.D.
- HAROLD MORRISON, M.D.
- WILLIAM REINHARDT, M.D.
- FREDERICK SHERWOOD, M.D.
- R. A. WEILERSTEIN, M.D.

HOUSE OFFICERS
- FREDERICK BECKERT, M.D.
- ARTHUR A. CIVELLO, M.D.
- FRANK HOLT, M.D.
- EDMUND D. JUNG, M.D.
- S. J. KARSANT, M.D.
- E. A. KIBRICK, M.D.
- CHARLES LENERT, M.D.
- E. P. LISTON, M.D.
- WILLIAM THOMAS, M.D.

First Fabiola Hospital directory plaque.

Dr. Morris Collen, December, 1968.

Morris Collen Comes to Permanente

Morrie Collen is a king among doctors. —Wallace Cooke, M.D., Kaiser Foundation Hospital/Walnut Creek, founding physician-in-chief and retired member of the Permanente Medical Group Executive Committee.

Morrie Collen is one of the smartest internists I've ever met, including all the men that I had in medical school. He equaled all of them and was a great teacher, a great man to work under. —Fred Pellegrin, M.D., Physician leader.

Dr. Collen's pioneering in medicine, cybernetics, automation, and computerization was responsible . . . for the recognition this organization received from all over the world and has certainly added to the reputation of our program. —Cecil Cutting, Permanente pioneer and first executive medical director of the Permanente Medical Group.

He is the most brilliant internist I've ever met in my whole medical career. —Carl Fisher, M.D., first Kaiser Permanente anesthesiologist.

One of the keys to the success of the Permanente Health Plan was the ability of its director, Sidney Garfield, to attract, recruit, and keep well-trained and conscientious physicians who would form a cadre of leaders within the new medical group. The standard of medical care provided by the physicians of Sidney Garfield and Associates was set very high.

On July 1, 1942, a man who would leave a deep and lasting imprint on the policy and standards of the Permanente Health Plan, arrived in Oakland. There is no way to understand and appreciate the history of the health plan and its contributions to American medicine without knowing about the contributions of Morris Collen, M.D.

July 1, 1942

Dr. Garfield had met Morris Collen at Los Angeles County Hospital. Garfield had just returned to Los Angeles after setting up the medical care program and hospital at Grand Coulee Dam. L.A. County Hospital, one of the nation's largest and finest, attracted some of the brightest medical graduates from around the country who had applied there for internships and residencies. Garfield, in his new capacity as "super resident" in surgery, had the opportunity to get to know these people in the best possible way—by working with them. Many of the physicians who would become leaders in the Permanente Medical Groups first met Dr. Garfield at L.A. County. Among them was Morris F. Collen, M.D.

Collen, a native of Minneapolis, had received an undergraduate degree in electrical engineering from the University of Minnesota. Originally he had intended to continue his studies combining engineering with biomedical research. Dr. Collen credits his change of career plans to a suggestion made by an attractive young Canadian nurse, Bobbie Diner, whom he was dating at the time. One month before graduation she said to him, "If you're going to get a Ph.D. and spend three years at it, why don't you go for an M.D.?" Dr. Collen must have appreciated her advice because he did enroll in medical school, and, during his senior year, the two eloped and were married.

By the end of a two-year internship at Michael Reese Hospital in Chicago, where, coincidentally, Sidney Garfield, had interned a few years earlier, the young physician had decided to specialize in internal medicine. He applied for residencies at the Mayo Clinic in Minnesota and at Los Angeles County Hospital. He was accepted by both. Since the position at his first choice, Mayo Clinic, did not open until the following January, and the L.A. County residency started in July, the young couple moved to Los Angeles. It may not have been their first choice, but at least they were getting away from those rugged Minnesota winters.

Later Dr. Collen recalled becoming acquainted with Dr. Garfield:

> *Sid was the supervisor in surgery for USC [University of Southern California, which staffed LA County Hospital], and the residents ran the hospital. The attending men would come, make rounds, and then they'd leave and we'd take care of the patients. Sid was very good and so that's how I got to know him. Whenever we needed a surgical consultation, I'd call him. It didn't happen often, but often enough that I got to know him and developed a great respect for him.*

When America entered the war, Dr. Collen knew that because of his bronchial asthma he wouldn't be drafted, but he was anxious to find a place to practice medicine where he could be helpful to the war effort. Another resident at the County Hospital, Irving Weisenfeld, mentioned that his friend Dr. Garfield had gone to Richmond to open an industrial program in the Kaiser shipyards. The two decided to find out more about it. Perhaps they could find interesting, useful work there.

Dr. Garfield took the two of them to lunch in the lush, Victorian-style Garden Court in San Francisco's luxurious Palace Hotel. Collen, still a self-described "small-town boy," was impressed by the surroundings as well as by the program outlined by Dr. Garfield. When Garfield asked him, "Would you like to join us as an internist?" Collen remembers replying immediately, "Gee, I'd be delighted." It was the beginning of an association with the Health Plan that continues to bring new credit to both Dr. Collen and to the medical care program.

When Collen began work on July 1, 1942, the Fabiola Hospital in Oakland had yet to open, and the patients the physicians were seeing at this time were almost all surgical, shipyard-accident victims. He recalls Garfield saying to him, "Go to the shipyard to see what you can do there." It turned out to be an inauspicious beginning.

"I went to the Richmond Field Hospital. . . . Bruce Henley was chief of surgery and I had no training in surgery. Patients would come in with injuries. I remember saying, 'Bruce, what do I do here?' At the end of the day Henley said, 'Coll, you're just no help. Get the hell out of here. We're too busy. Go back and tell Cutting [Cecil Cutting, chief of staff, who was running the day-to-day operations of the medical group] we can't use you.'"

For awhile, Collen, the internist, had to be content with doing mundane tasks such as preoperative examinations, but when the Fabiola Hospital opened in August and the program had hospital beds of its own, he was able to begin using his training more effectively.

From the start, Dr. Collen was anxious to tie his experience with patients to clinical research. The heavy equipment, massive loads, and unskilled labor force in the shipyards gave him his first opportunity: ". . . the first patient I saw in the hospital was this man with spots on his chest, petechiae. The only cases like this I'd seen were meningococcemia, very sick patients. A truck had ridden over him and fractured both his femurs." A natural teacher, Dr. Collen goes on to explain:

> *What happens is that when you fracture the long bones and crush them enough, the fat in the marrow breaks down, goes into the circulation, and when the little fat globules get to an end capillary, [they] rupture. And so you see these little spots in the skin. When the fat droplets go to the lungs, they block the lung capillaries, and you get changes in the x-ray that look like pneumonia, with right-heart failure. ... We had several such cases and I wrote a paper on it.*

As busy as he was, with too few physicians taking care of the rapidly expanding shipyard workforce, made up mostly of people who were too old or too sick for military service, Dr. Collen found time to write a paper on a series of patients he saw with this particular, somewhat unusual problem. Although he had already published papers while at L.A. County Hospital, this was the first of scores of articles, papers and books he would write, bringing credit not just to himself but to the entire medical care program

Early on, Dr. Garfield recognized Collen's potential as a leader, although Collen's first "promotion" came about in a very informal manner. Dr. Collen enjoys retelling the story with self-deprecating humor:

"I was the first internist, and we got very, very busy. I went to Sidney and said; 'I can't be on twenty-four hours a day seven days a week, I need help.' Sidney said, 'Fine, we'll get some internists.' I said, 'Will you write them letters?' He said, 'I don't have time, you write them.'

"'Ok I'll write them letters and I'll bring them to you and you'll sign them?'
"And he said, 'No, I don't have time, you sign them.'
"I asked him, 'How do you want me to sign them?' There was a long pause, and he said, 'Sign them, Chief of Medicine.' And that was how I got to be Chief of Medicine. I always tell the story and say, 'If you want to be an easy chief, be the first guy on the job.'"

Sixty years after he began working with the Permanente Health Plan, Dr. Collen left no doubt that he was well-satisfied with how he spent his life: "Students will often ask me, 'Would you advise me to go to medical school?' I answer, 'If there is such a thing as reincarnation, I would again go to medical school, and then apply for a job as a Permanente physician.'"

This poster (circa 1943) encouraged shipyard workers to sign up for the Health Plan, a bargain at fifty cents a week.

The Shipyard Health Plan in Operation: 1942

Thousands of men were already turning out ships from Yard No. 1 and construction crews were building a second yard of similar size alongside it. Meanwhile, Henry Kaiser had just signed a contract to build a third yard. Already 30,000 men at were at work in the shipyard complex and the number was growing rapidly as workers streaming into Richmond were being hired almost as fast as they could fill in the paperwork.

The rapid growth of the shipyard work force meant there was an increasingly urgent need for more facilities to take care of the inevitable illnesses and injuries. No sooner had the renovated 54-bed Fabiola Hospital opened than it was swamped with patients and expansion began. Three new hospital wings were added, one after the other.

Physician-founder Sidney Garfield considered the 1942-beginning of shipyard medical care as the founding of Kaiser Permanente. However, from the vantage point of the present, it appears that the more significant year is 1945, when the shipyard Health Plan was opened to the public. In any case, the postwar plan was built on a foundation made up of the experience of the dedicated group of physicians and administrators who had been through the wartime years with Garfield and Kaiser and were convinced that a prepaid, multi-specialty, group practice was an excellent way to provide health care. Nevertheless, 1942 saw the beginnings of the Permanente Health Plan and the Permanente Foundations as well as the opening of the first Permanente

Hospital (Fabiola). Here is how some of the people who were there, fashioning what would become Kaiser Permanente, remember "the time before the beginning."

Dr. Cutting, one of the founding physicians of the Permanente Medical Group, remembers how "twenty-four hours a day, buses shuttled in a circular route from one First Aid station to another in the shipyards, picking up sick and injured workers." Every twenty minutes one of those shipyard buses would arrive at the Richmond Field Hospital, disgorging another group of workers needing treatment. Because so many of the workers had already been rejected by the military as being medically unfit for the armed services, Dr. Cutting described the work force as a "walking pathological museum."

Physician Norman Haugen came to the Permanente Health Plan from the University of California San Francisco as a resident in 1942. Since it was important to be able to examine and treat patients as quickly and efficiently as possible, Dr. Haugen helped to design an ingenious combination physician's desk, examination table, and wash stand that was at the heart of the Field Hospital's surgery clinic.

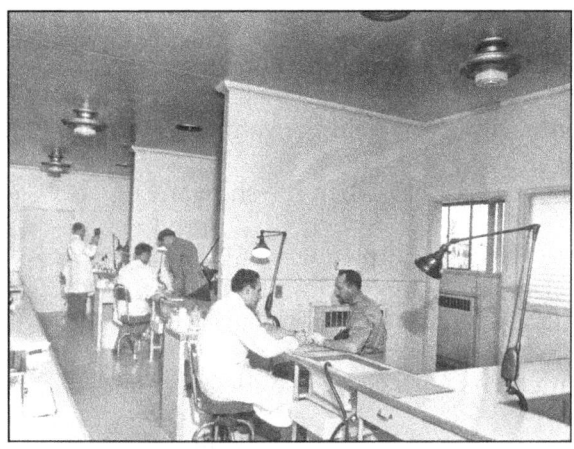

An ingenious combination physician's desk, exam table, and washstand. Designed by Permanente doctors to treat workers efficiently in the limited space of the new hospital. Common materials needed by the physicians were at close hand in cabinets behind them.

According to Dr. Haugen:

"It was really an interesting arrangement. There was a continuous bench about fifty feet long and periodically there was an opening with a hinge. If a patient came and had his foot injured, you needed to look at his foot. You could lift this section up, pull out a bar and he could put his foot on it. About every six or eight feet this table would have a 'T' extension, big enough so that he could lie down. And there would be curtains there so if you wanted to examine somebody for a hernia or hemorrhoids or something, why, he could lie down on this."

Meanwhile, nurses helped organize the flow of patients through the clinics. They comforted those in pain and set up examination rooms for those patients who needed added privacy. They also saw that doctors had the necessary supplies near at hand when they called for them. With the help of the nursing staff, the physicians treated, on the average, four patients an hour during ten- to twelve-hour days.

The dispensing of medications was also streamlined. The Health Plan coded the most common medications so physicians didn't waste any time writing out the name of a drug on a prescription pad. For instance, aspirin was "#1," and "#5" was a mixture of phenobarbital and belladonna, used to treat common stomach problems. The doctors had sets of stamps with prescription numbers on them. That and the name of the patient was all that was needed on the prescription—no drug name, no M.D. name. It was fast and it was efficient. The doctors grew to like the system, but it was stopped after the war when outside pressure made the Plan conform to standard pharmaceutical practice.

Sometimes more than medical science was considered in prescribing medication. Prescription "#1," aspirin, came in two versions, "1A" and "1B." "1A" was the common white aspirin; "1B" was the identical aspirin but pink. A physician, under appropriate circumstances, could say to a patient, "These aren't working? Try these pink ones. We find that they're often effective when the white ones aren't."

Up to ten ambulances were available to move the injured from the shipyards to the hospital. Most stood idle but there was always the possibility of an accident that injured a group of workers, all of whom would need to be transported to hospitals. Luckily, although serious accidents took place, they almost always involved only one or maybe two workers. Cecil Cutting did remember one particular ship launching, though, when a group of enthusiastic workers and spectators climbed onto the roof of a shed to get a better look at the ceremonies. The shed wasn't strong enough to function as a celebratory grandstand. It collapsed, sending a dozen people to the hospital.

Although very few workers had any shipyard experience, and most had never even worked around heavy construction equipment, there were few serious accidents. This was due in large part to an unrelenting emphasis on workplace safety. Even so, there was always a steady flow of injured workers requiring treatment. When Norman Haugen arrived at Permanente, he came with a young surgeon, his friend Donald Grant. Dr. Grant remembers treating a lot of burns: ". . . they've got a welding torch, the torch going down part of a wall of a ship and there's somebody working on the other side. There's a hole. The welding torch gets the one on the other side." Dr. Grant remembers a lot of crushing injuries, too. "We had a bunch of [shipyard workers] who were walking under a big plate of metal, being carried on these overhead cranes—walking under to keep out of the rain. And that broke."

Because of the sheer number of workers and variety of injuries, physicians underwent a period of rapid learning. From their experience they developed innovative treatments and a body of knowledge that they shared with other physicians, not just among themselves but with others in their profession.. The treatment of pneumonia is just a prime example of the many contributions made by Permanente physicians.

In the days before penicillin was available, pneumonia was a virulent killer, and the disease was rampant around the shipyards. There were several reasons for this. One was the effect of Northern California's rainy winters on the lungs of people not used to working outdoors, around the clock, in cold and wet weather. Making matters worse was that the winter of 1942-43 was one of the coldest and rainiest on record.

Another contributing factor was the poor health of many workers: most of the men were too old, too young, or already too unhealthy for military duty, and many arrived with chronic health problems. Added to this was the fact that living conditions for many of the workers could only be described as wretched. The Kaiser company, as well as municipal and federal authorities, rushed to get housing ready for the flood of workers, but supply could not keep up with demand. Families were living in unheated shacks, in condemned buildings, even in abandoned automobiles. Dr. Grant remembers when he and Dr. Phil Raimondi (another of the physicians who would stay on after the war) admitted twenty pneumonia patients in a single night.

Dr. Collen, who by that time was chief of medicine, remembers those days before penicillin:

> *It was cold and damp in the shipyards, and they'd get pneumococcal pneumonias and they would die. All we had in the early days was horse serum, but horse serum would give them reactions, serum sickness. . . . On the second or third floor of the Fabiola Hospital I had a dozen or so beds and they were mostly pneumonia patients. Then as we got busier, I got some fifty or sixty beds on C. [C Wing was the third addition to the main building.] We had ninety patients with pneumonia at one time, so, on the first floor of the Fabiola building, in a room that had been our library, we put mattresses on the floor with orange boxes as bedside tables. We overflowed to the first floor and to the basement floor of the Fabiola hospital.*

Dr. Grant described how Morrie Collen had organized the care of the pneumonia patients. "He arranged things by step 1, 2, 3, 4, 5 to help us take care of these things. You would get a diagnosis of lobar pneumonia. You would type the information on a form. If it's 1, 2, 3, you do such and such. If it's 1, 2 and 4, you do such. If it's 3, you've got to do something different. If that doesn't respond, you do thus-and-so, just like that. . . . To have this all classified was very helpful."

Soon, the Fabiola Hospital had the largest pneumonia service in the country. Doctors' rounds sometimes took from eight in the morning until two in the afternoon to complete. Antibiotics were still years away, but newer medications, sulfa drugs that were more effective than horse serum, had become available. The problem with sulfa drugs, however, was that they were complex to administer and the possibilities for complications many. Dr. Collen and the physicians on his staff were seeing so many pneumonia cases that they developed expertise with the difficult sulfa drugs that was nationally recognized as being unmatched. They were saving more of these critically-ill patients than anyone else; the mortality rate dropped to an astounding one-half of what it was at the nearby San Francisco County Hospital. As a result, the wartime industrial medical program centered in Oakland earned a national reputation as a leader in the treatment of pneumonia.

Medical schools began applying to have their interns rotate through this medical service so they could learn the Kaiser protocol. Many physicians who attended the University of California Medical School during this time were very pleased to have had part of their training as interns or residents under Dr. Collen. Their participation was a significant vote of confidence in the Permanente medical program. (Later, though, during the bitter years when Kaiser Permanente was seen as a threat to the fee-for-service medical community and when hostility was at its height, these physicians were less willing to admit the value of that training.)

As he would do over and over again during a long and distinguished career as a clinician and a researcher, Dr. Collen described his experience in well-written medical journal articles for the medical community at large. A *New England Journal of Medicine* review of Dr. Collen's article about the epidemiology and management of over 800 cases of pneumonia concluded that: "These low fatality rates suggest that the conditions to which the shipyard workers were exposed did not aggravate the prognosis in those who acquired the pneumonia. More likely, it reflects the fine type of medical care that these patients received." This final sentence gave the fledgling medical program good reason for pride in its achievements.

An advantage of a health plan having a large membership is the possibility of using medical records to measure the effectiveness of treatments. Dr. Collen followed up his article on pneumonia with a book on the treatment of pneumonia based on the documentation of the hundreds of cases. After the war Dr. Cecil Cutting and two of his Permanente colleagues published an article in a medical journal (*California and Western Medicine*) reviewing treatment of the 13,000 fractures they handled during the war.

In 1943, medicine was changing, and Permanente was on the leading edge. At that time, 90 percent of what little penicillin was available went to the Armed Services. However, Permanente physicians received one of the first doses of penicillin distributed to civilians on the West Coast. Dr. Collen recalls, "We received the very small dose of only 15,000 units of penicillin that we gave to a very sick patient with type VII pneumococcic pneumonia whom we did not expect to survive. To our surprise and delight, he recovered completely; we thought it was indeed a miracle drug."

There was more to treat than just injuries and pneumonias. Permanente physicians saw a wide variety of conditions ranging from polio and typhoid to hernias and an epidemic of conjunctivitis. There was even a series of leprosy cases. Inevitably, there were a lot of just plain odd cases, too.

"I remember a woman coming in," Dr. Grant recalled. "She and her girlfriend had been sitting at a bar drinking and all of a sudden they got in an argument. One of them said to the other, 'I don't like you,' grabbed her ears and bit off her nose. And once I pulled the heel of a high-heeled shoe out of a scalp."

One of the most puzzling conditions the doctors saw was what the welders called "Monday Morning Fever." After a day off, some welders would become ill when they returned to work. They would show up at the clinic with fever, chills, and nausea. They were clearly sick. The fever would pass fairly quickly, and the welders would go back to work without any more symptoms until after their next day off. It was a real puzzlement. The physicians were stymied until Dr. Cutting and his colleagues finally figured out that the culprit was zinc fumes. During welding down in the hulls, a high concentration of zinc fumes would form in the still air and some people were very sensitive to them. These were the people who would come down with "Monday Morning Fever." Over the course of the work week, their bodies adjusted to the zinc, but after one or two days off, their tolerance disappeared and they would become sick again.

Probably the most common surgical procedure was hernia repair. Dr. Haugen explained: "During the 1920s and 1930s, hernias were repaired with absorbable sutures. The recurrence rate was just terrible." Hernia repairs were not expected to be permanent. A man age thirty-five who had a hernia operation would expect to have several more in his lifetime. The Permanente physicians decided to try something different. "Dr. [Bruce] Henley, and I suppose Dr. Cutting was involved, too, decided to use nonabsorbable sutures. We just went down to the dry goods store and bought J.P. Coates #40 and #30 cotton thread, put them on rubber spools, and sterilized them." It even turned out to make a better suture.

Another innovation was how long these surgical patients were kept in bed after their operations. "It was the practice to keep them in bed for fourteen days. The trouble was that every once in a while one of those fellows, after being in bed for fourteen days, stood up and just dropped dead from a pulmonary embolus. Then we started getting them out of bed early, usually got them out of bed the next day." This protocol saved lives and soon became general practice.

Dr. Haugen went on to say that even though many of the hernias were clearly pre-existing conditions, if a worker claimed it was an industrial injury, the Health Plan was pretty liberal about treatment. What was important was getting people back to work. The insurance companies cooperated, too.

> *Just across the street from the hospital there was Hartford Insurance Company run by A.B. Martin, and Industrial Indemnity had an adjusting office over there. They were very generous. Somebody would come in to make a claim. Bernice Terkovich was a crackerjack stenographer, one of those old fashioned stenographers who could take shorthand as fast as you could talk. She'd come back with a letter typed up and you'd say, "Did I say that?" She had edited it with better English than you'd used and punctuated it nicely. We'd give the patient the letter and he'd go across the street to Industrial Indemnity or Hartford Insurance Company. The indemnity companies decided whether or not they wanted to accept it. When the patient came back, we'd put him on a schedule, probably for next morning.*

When workers signed on at the Richmond shipyards, they automatically received coverage in the Health Plan, but under Workman's Compensation that coverage was only for work-related sicknesses or injuries. They were encouraged to spend an additional fifty cents per week for full coverage, and more than 90 percent did. Those first Health Plan members made good use of their comprehensive coverage. For one thing, the long hours and heavy labor led to a lot of automobile accidents. Dr. George Gara, an Italian-trained Hungarian physician, who found himself stranded in San Francisco when the United States went to war and who joined Garfield's group, remembered the car-crash victims. "These most often came in at night. Workers who commuted and who had an accident, they would all come back to Permanente."

Not all medical care was dispensed at the two hospitals. Each of the shipyards had a firstaid station. Most of the injured workers seen at the first aid station had cuts and bruises. More serious wounds went directly to a hospital. A very common injury was something called a "flash burn." Welders' torches burned with such an intense light that it could damage the surface of an unprotected eye. Welders had smoked-glass goggles, and they soon learned not to fire up their torches until they had placed their goggles over their eyes. However, in the crowded work areas, a nearby welder might light up unexpectedly and the flash from the torch, even off to the side, could cause a painful burn on the eyeball.

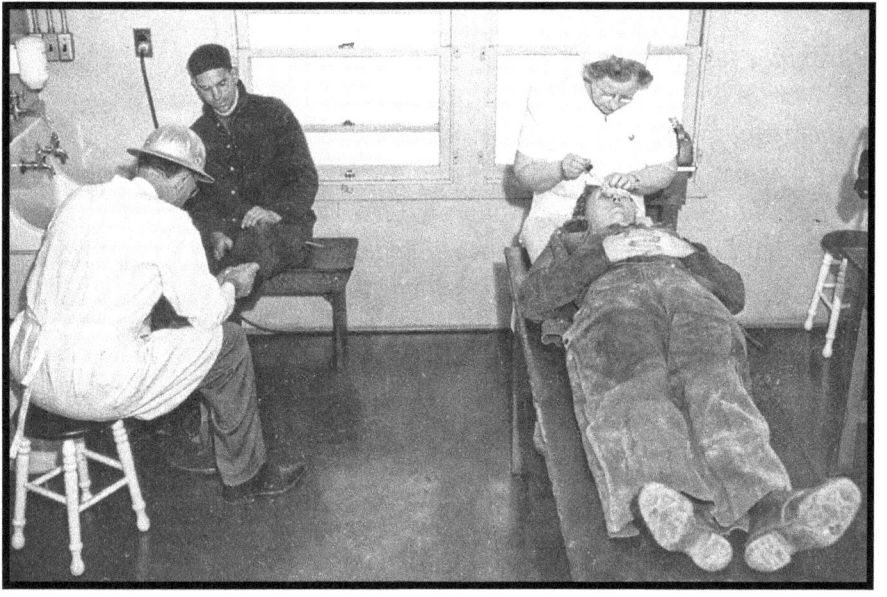

First aid room with two workers, one of whom gets an eyewash treatment for a flash burn.

For flash-burn cases, the first aid station had a separate room with six gurneys. Nurse Harriet Stewart remembered: "We'd put Novocain in their eyes . . . and put a wet pack on for awhile." Unless it was a severe burn, in about an hour the welder returned to work. A war was going on. Workers and health staff never lost sight of the fact that their responsibility during this time of crisis was simply, "Build Ships."

Explaining *Permanente*

Because of the success of the Kaiser Permanente model of health insurance and health care delivery, it is hard to remember just how unusual such a system was more than sixty years ago. It was a concept not well understood even by many of the subscribers at the time. Most of the Kaiser shipyard workers only learned how valuable their coverage was when they were unfortunate enough to need it. The "four bits" paid to the Permanente Health Plan each week meant the worker, in addition to receiving Workmen's Compensation, also had comprehensive health care coverage for almost every sort of nonwork-related sickness or injury. Then, as now, it was important that a broad base of workers subscribe to the plan.

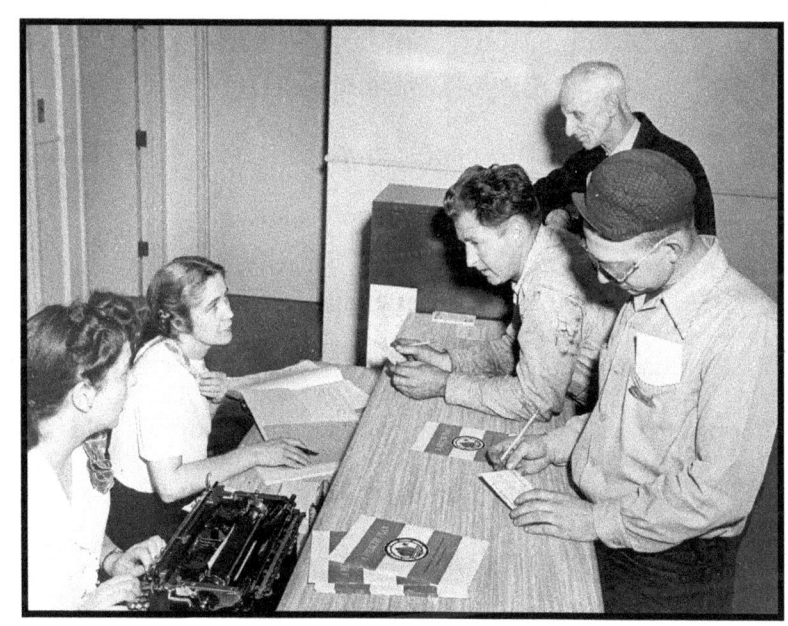

Signing up for the Permanente Health Plan.

The Health Plan, in order to survive and to flourish, needed to make sure that shipyard workers understood what they were getting for their voluntary fifty-cents-a-week dues. To hammer this home, shipyard magazines often carried not just health and safety tips but also articles to help employees understand how sharing the risk worked to their benefit. and how the Health Plan was valuable to them, even when they did not seem to be using it. For instance, one winter issue of *Fore 'N' Aft* carried a partial list of what the combined fifty-cents-a-week dues of the tens of thousands of shipyard workers had purchased in one year:

1,373,611 treatments

5,000 surgical operations

82,870 physiotherapy treatments

81,940 laboratory tests

181,487 bottles of aspirin

136,549 bottles of cough syrup

39,297 bottles of nose drops

19,262 bottles of throat gargle

12,739 bottles of liniment

11,487 bottles of antacid

3,104 bottles of calamine lotion

9,987 tubes of eye ointment

9,024 packages of analgesic balm

7,629 inhalator bottles

31,151 packages of sulfa drugs

In the same issue a letter appeared from an anonymous Permanente physician emphasizing the value of the fifty-cents-a-week dues as well as the satisfaction that physicians felt at being able to play an important role in building the "bridge of ships" so important to the war effort. More than sixty years later, some of that doctor's language still sounds familiar.

Dear Fellow-Shipbuilders:

You may object to a doctor calling himself a shipbuilder—but I like to think that by guarding the health of shipbuilders I am indirectly building ships, too. I recently saw the total figures representing the services rendered by YOUR Health Plan in the first year of operation. These statistics illustrate plainly the tremendous volume of medical services you men and women are buying for yourselves at fifty cents a week. We doctors are proud to be able to serve the war effort and safeguard your health in this way.

We are also proud to be a part of this wonderful new progressive Health Plan. A doctor, like any other craftsman, prefers to be associated with capable well-trained men. Here we have this opportunity. Some of our doctors have come to us directly from their hospital training and others have given up private practice to join our ranks. Each of our specialists has had years of specialized training at an excellent medical teaching center. Likewise, our nurses are all fully trained registered nurses and our First Aid men and technicians are all well-qualified. Considering the scarcity of trained medical personnel, this is quite an accomplishment.

Many prominent civil, military and government authorities have told us that the facilities are excellent. However, we realize that our facilities are too small, and are expanding as rapidly as possible. We recognize that pleasant surroundings have much to do with an invalid's happiness.

But the most important thing to remember is that this is YOUR Health Plan. When you set foot in one of these hospitals it is YOUR hospital that you and 69,999 others are paying for at the rate of fifty cents per week.

We get many fine compliments, and—believe me—we love it. We also listen carefully to the complaints we hear about the hospitals, both in Oakland and in Richmond. It is true that sometimes there are waits at the hospital. But please remember that while you are waiting to see your doctor, he is serving one of your fellow workers who is also sick and perhaps sicker than you. In no instance is a real emergency kept waiting. We would rather keep five people waiting than jeopardize an urgent case that needs immediate attention.

Sincerely,

A Permanente staff doctor

A testimonial from a shipyard employee to the editors of Fore 'N' Aft about how well the Health Plan had worked for him reads:

"On the way to work a month ago, a heart attack landed me in the Emergency Hospital in San Francisco. At first I was rather ignored but when they learned I belonged to the shipyard Health Plan, things took winged action. Soon a shipyard ambulance had me in the Permanente Hospital in Oakland. Every day, a Health Plan representative called to see if there was some little act of kindness they could do. And the checking and care I received there could not have been better if I had been Henry Ford."

To this bit of praise, the editor had added only one remark;

"Dr. Garfield, stop blushing."

Health and Safety *Messages*

KEEP FIT THIS WINTER

WEAR WARM CLOTHING
If you work out of doors, wear a slicker or water-repellant clothing. Dress warmly and keep your feet dry. A good pair of work shoes, coated with grease to make them waterproof is a good health investment.

GET MEDICAL TREATMENT
If you feel a cold coming on, go to your First Aid station immediately. Skilled doctors and nurses can usually give you treatment and help you stop your cold or throat infection before it goes too far.

GET PLENTY OF REST...
Complete rest is your best bet in getting rid of colds and infections. Give your body a fighting chance to lick illness by getting enough sleep. Nature is the best cure for minor illnesses, but you've got to give her a chance.

EAT RIGHT...
Eat lots of fruits and vegetables. Yellow vegetables like carrots and squash are rich in preventative Vitamin A. Citrus fruits will give you the Vitamin C you need, and plenty of milk, eggs and butter will help build resistance.

YOUR HEALTH IS A VITAL WAR WEAPON

This page appeared as the back cover of a Fore 'N' Aft, *the shipyard magazine. Reducing sick days was one of the ways for management to keep production up. It was also "the right thing" to do. Prevention was always an important element in the prepaid medical program.*

Not flu shots, but blustery winds and raw, rainy weather, the main ingredients of winters in Northern California, were the reason for reminders such as this in the *Fore 'N' Aft* weekly magazine. Every issue devoted a page to health and safety. Although the subjects were serious, they were most often presented with humor.

How Henry J. Kaiser and the Rosies Helped Win World War II

The "Safety Boner" Contest

It is possible that this poster reminded Dr. Garfield of his days on the Mojave desert, where his hospital's conversion to prepayment had made him realize that an emphasis on worksite safety could be a great benefit both to him and to the people he took care of. Now, just ten years later, he was responsible for the care of nearly 200,000 people, and on-the-job-safety education needed to be carried out on a huge scale.

As part of a safety campaign, the artist crammed as many unsafe activities into this cartoon as he and the safety engineers could imagine. They came up with 112 and ran a contest to see if anyone could spot them all. The level of safety awareness in the shipyards was so high that the winner actually found 118, including the six unintended "safety boners," and the judges had to agree she was right!

Working in close quarters, the stress of long hours, the large number of people whose health to some extent was already compromised, and the prevalence of bad habits such as spitting on the floor or decks combined to increase vulnerability to tuberculosis, even today a serious disease. The Permanente Health Plan campaign to curb its spread included free chest x-rays, originally provided in cooperation with the Contra Costa County TB Association, tips on protecting oneself from the disease, and periodic screening. Eventually the Richmond Field Hospital acquired its own x-ray machine in order to carry on a continuous screening program for shipyard workers.

The physician reading chest x-rays is identified as "Dr. Clinton." Some years ago, I received a letter from a man looking for information about his mother, who had worked at the Richmond Field Hospital. He was very proud of her participation in the war effort. At the time, I hadn't been able to help him, but as I was going through some *Fore 'N' Afts*, which I had recently purchased from the family of a former shipyard worker,

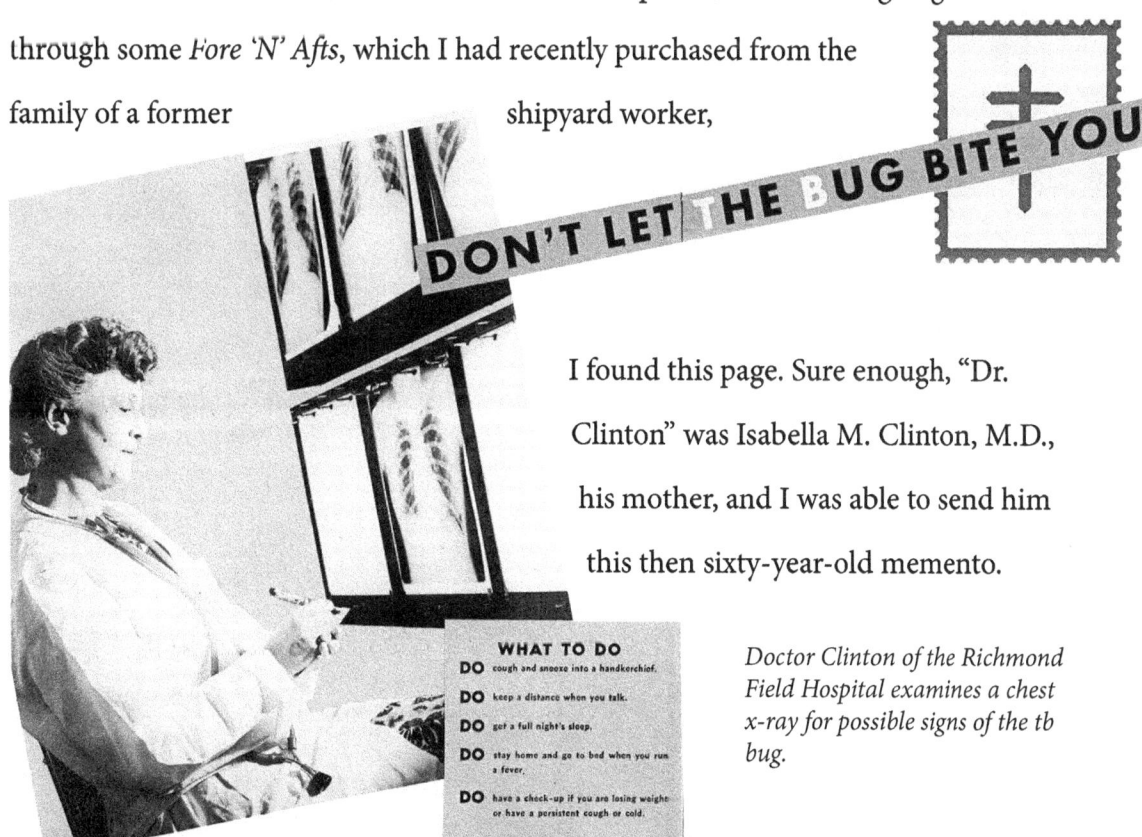

I found this page. Sure enough, "Dr. Clinton" was Isabella M. Clinton, M.D., his mother, and I was able to send him this then sixty-year-old memento.

Doctor Clinton of the Richmond Field Hospital examines a chest x-ray for possible signs of the tb bug.

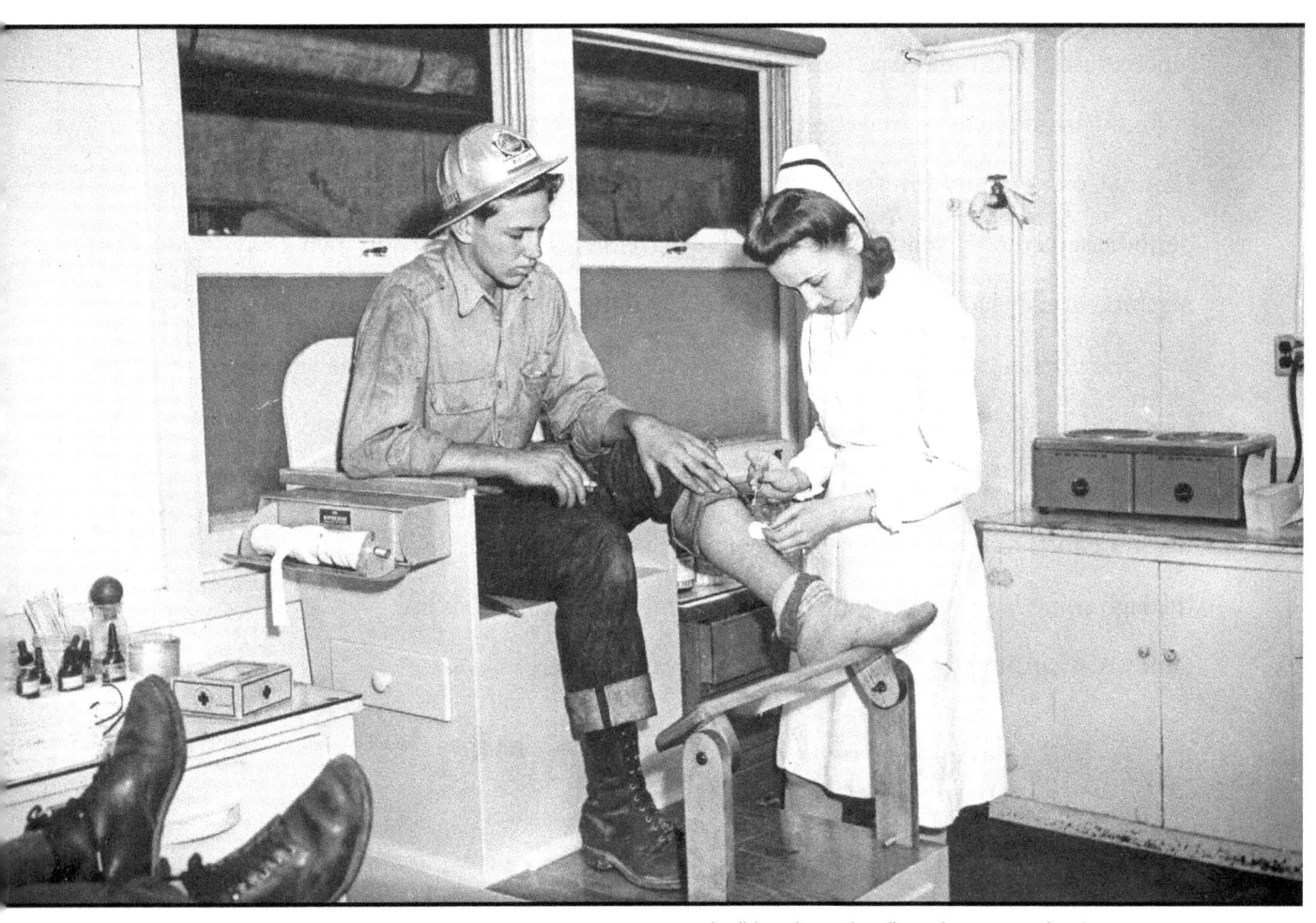

The "shoeshine chair" made it easier for the nurses, "so we didn't have to stoop over to wrap ankles and things."

Shipyard Nurse

It is a surprise for many people to learn that the first women working in the Kaiser shipyards were not there to build ships. They were nurses who worked in first aid stations placed strategically throughout the yards. When the nurses came to the shipyards, no one was sure what the effect on the men would be. One of those nurses, Harriet Stewart, retired after forty-seven years with Kaiser Permanente, had memories of those wartime years which she wanted to share. Along with Tom Debley, director of the Heritage Resources Department of Kaiser Permanente, I visited with her in her Richmond home. In that conversation and the several that followed, she recalled her experiences. They offer a rare and sometimes amusing insight into what it was like for those first medical Rosies.

In early 1942, not long after Pearl Harbor, Harriet Stewart, a recent graduate from the nursing program at Creighton College (now Creighton University) in Omaha, Nebraska, went off to Los Angeles. After a few months working at the Good Samaritan Hospital, she heard from friends working at the Kaiser shipyards in Richmond. They described the shipyards as an exciting place to work and, unlike Good Samaritan Hospital, it was tied directly to the war effort. She thought it sounded interesting and exciting.

In June 1942, the shipyard medical care program was still so new that there were neither hospital nor medical offices. Harriet Stewart's interview took place in a rented physician's office on "Pill Hill" in Oakland where sick and injured shipyard workers went for treatment until new facilities at the shipyards would be ready. In a waiting room that was so sparsely furnished that there was no table, she filled out the application on her lap. The nurse who interviewed her was Millie Cutting, wife of one of the key physicians in the new medical group. Although she did not have the title, Nurse Cutting was acting as the head of nursing. The interview lasted only a few minutes. Millie Cutting, satisfied that the young nurse would be a valuable addition to the medical staff, wasted no time and asked her, "Can you go to work this afternoon in Yard One?"

Harriet could, and a few minutes later, the newly hired nurse was on a local bus heading the few miles to Richmond and the shipyards. There she had her photograph taken, received her ID badge, and was escorted directly to the Yard One first aid station staffed by one doctor, three nurses, and two first aid men. She recalled, "Our little building was only about a hundred feet from where they launched the boats, so we were right down on the water." The location gave her the opportunity to see several launchings. On launching days, "there was a lot of commotion. There were people coming and going in cars bringing the people for the launching . . . a governor or governor's wife, or a mayor from someplace, or a high official. And they were treated with—oh, awe. The launchings were around eleven-thirty, so there was always a big meal for them somewhere but not in the shipyard."

It seemed to the young nurse that the first aid waiting room was always crowded. Injured men registered at the front desk ". . . and

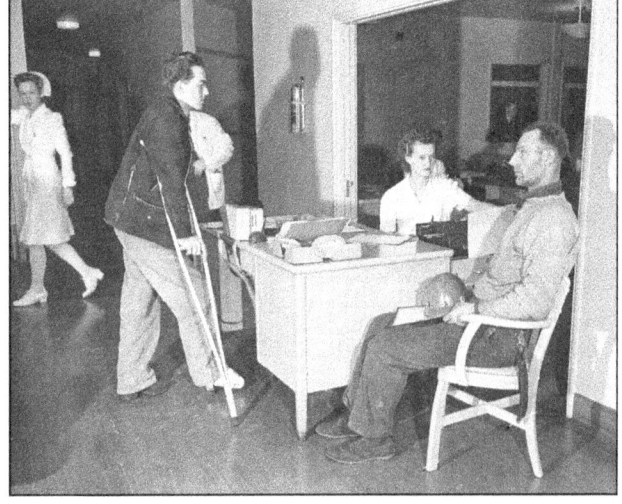

Injured workers at front desk.

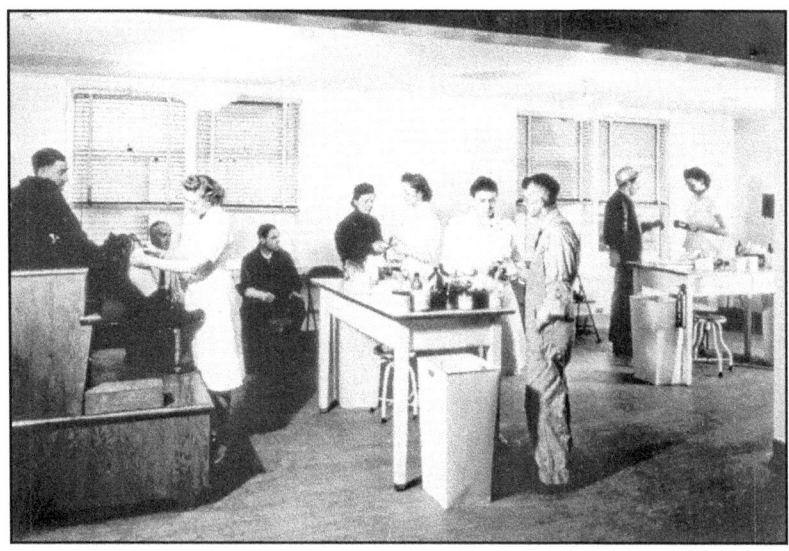

Inside busy shipyard first aid station: at left, utilizing the "shoeshine" chair.

then sat down in the seat until we could take care of them in the next room. In the treatment room we had a row of six chairs. The middle one was built up like a shoeshine boy, so that we didn't have to stoop over it to wrap ankles and things." She noted how different medicine had been at that time. "There was only one sink in that room. The men that needed care, if they had blood on their hands, they washed in that sink and we washed in that sink. Never thought anything about it. Then they sat down, and we took care of them." One man, who came in with a serious scrape on his leg, kept returning even after the leg had healed. He got special attention. Several months later he and Harriet were married.

Especially at the beginning, nurses enjoyed a unique place in the social structure of the shipyard. "We were the only women allowed in the shipyard. The office help

Nursing staff in front of Richmond Field Hospital.

was outside the gate. We had respect like you wouldn't believe. We wore nurses' uniforms, nurses' hats, white shoes, and we conducted ourselves like we were taught in training—you know—ladies."

Nurse Stewart remembers, though, that the first women hired as shipbuilders, in late summer 1942, were treated differently than the nurses had been when they arrived. The men resented these new women's presence. By chance, Harriet Stewart learned about that firsthand. Each day, a group of men would eat their lunch on the ground in the shade of the first aid building and through the open window, Stewart and the other nurses could hear them talk. Their evaluation of the new women workers was scathing. "They're no good. They can't perform." If a woman carpenter had a hammer on the side of her coveralls, or if she was carrying a saw and walked by, the men laughed openly at her, saying loudly such things as, "She doesn't even know what to do with those tools." Nurse Stewart remembered, though, that this abuse didn't last. "Rosies" were proving their ability to do the work that needed to be done and they earned the respect of their fellow workers, at least to the extent that much of the outright taunts and derisive comments faded away.

Many of the new workers flooding into the expanding shipyards were African Americans. Although they faced intolerance from other workers, Stewart proudly pointed out that there was no discrimination in the medical program. Patients were treated in order without regard to their ethnicity. "There was no discrimination of any sort in our care. If they were sick and they needed care, they were given exactly the care that the white men were given, and with respect. And that was that."

Permanente Patient—
Permanente Medicine

Lili Vickerson was a young nurse who came down to Richmond, California, from Canada for a job in the Kaiser shipyards. In the year she worked at the eye clinic in the Yard No. 1 first aid station, she made many friends among the other nurses and staff.

In October 1943, Lili was working the day shift, and at the end of her workday, 4:00 p.m., along with thousands of others, she made her way through the shipyard gate, past the security guards and out onto Cutting Boulevard. She hurried a little in order to get across the train tracks, which ran by the gate, before she would be blocked by the trolley coming down the tracks.

The trolley was an import. Not long before, the Second Avenue El, an aging elevated railway in New York City built in 1880, had been torn down. When there was a sudden need for a transportation system to get thousands of workers to and from the Richmond shipyards, the old New York trolley cars were shipped west and pressed into wartime service.*

As Lili Vickerson stepped across the rails that afternoon, she stumbled and was unable to recover and get out of the way before the trolley hit her. The trolley motorman slammed on the brakes. The steel wheels screeched against the tracks as

---

* Today, the lone survivor of the shipyard trolley system that began life in the 1890s in New York City as the Second Avenue Elevated Railway, or "El," continues to run over Northern California rails. Instead of carrying workers to the shipyards, the oldest electric-powered trolley in North America is now a working exhibit at the Western Railway Museum at Rio Vista Junction, California.

they tried to hold back the weight of the train of cars behind. That sound and the screams of horrified onlookers alerted security guard, George Payne, who sprinted towards Vickerson. Her leg had been horribly mangled, but Payne managed to snatch her head and shoulders away from the track, preventing her from being dragged under the wheels and crushed.

Someone called for an ambulance and within minutes Nurse Vickerson was being rushed to the Permanente Fabiola Hospital in Oakland.

Cecil Cutting, the surgeon who had begun working with Dr. Garfield at Grand Coulee Dam, was now chief of staff of both the Richmond and Oakland hospitals. In addition to his administrative duties, he was also a very busy surgeon. On that particular

Shipyard workers lined up to board trolley at night. The trolley was an import. Not long before, the recently dismantled Second Avenue El, an aging elevated railway in New York City, built in 1880, had been torn down.

afternoon, he was just finishing a long day in the operating rooms at Fabiola when he heard that a Permanente nurse had been seriously injured. He immediately scrubbed up for another operation and called together the best team available. As soon as he examined her, he knew he had no choice but to amputate the crushed leg.

Word of the accident spread rapidly through the medical care program. Along with it went the story of how the chief of staff had remained at the hospital in order to make sure personally that Lili Vickerson received the best possible care. Nurse Harriet

Stewart had worked with Vickerson at the Yard One first aid station. She remembers with much feeling that "What Dr. Cutting did meant an awful lot to the medical staff." At a time when everyone was being called on to make sacrifices, to work long hours, Cecil Cutting's example helped to cement the strong family feeling that grew up in the medical care program as well as among the shipyard workers during the war years.

When there was a sudden need for transportation to get thousands of workers to and from the Richmond shipyards, the old New York trolley cars were shipped west and pressed into wartime service.

Lili Vickerson had no family in the area, so her fellow shipyard nurses volunteered to give her special duty care at the hospital during the first weeks of her recovery so she would have friends with her during this difficult time. The injured nurse also faced the problem of how, once she was ready to leave the hospital, she was going to support herself. She was worried that even with the artificial leg she would be getting and with rehabilitation, she wouldn't be able to carry out the strenuous duties of nursing. Harriet Stewart remembered how relieved Vickerson was, and how appreciative her colleagues were, when they heard that Cecil Cutting promised that he would find a useful job for her and that she could have it for as long as she wanted. The job turned out to be supervisor at the Blood Bank in Oakland. There Lili Vickerson remained for many years putting her training and her experience to excellent use.

Beatrice Lei:

the First Woman Physician in the Permanente Medical Group

Beatrice Lei, M.D.

It is often said that the best way to tell a story is to begin at the beginning. The catch is that sometimes it is hard to tell just where "the beginning" is. In the case of Beatrice Lei, the first woman to become a partner of the Permanente Medical Group, the beginning might be considered to be in China in the middle of the nineteenth century, at the end of the Opium Wars. At that time Western nations forced open a number of Chinese ports in order to facilitate international trade, whether the inhabitants liked it or not. One of those ports, Shantou (Swatow), was not much more than a village in South China, but it had an excellent harbor as well as a navigable river that connected it to the country's interior. Soon Shantou prospered and grew. First came the military, followed by the missionaries. By the early twentieth century, Shantou had become a busy, cosmopolitan port city doing business with ships from all over the world.

That was the world into which Beatrice was born on April 10, 1910. She was the sixth child of a family that eventually numbered eleven children. At the time, her father was a lumber dealer and an entrepreneur. Later he started a fabric company and prospered well enough that he was able to build a Christian church for his community.

---

* Much of the material in this article comes from my interview with Dr. Lei's Chinese-speaking niece Jennie Li and from an undated interview of the late Dr. Lei in the Kaiser Permanente Heritage Resource Department. Ron Knox, vice president, Diversity at Kaiser Permanente, kindly arranged my interview. Gayle Tang patiently and carefully acted as translator.

During this period it was unusual for a young girl to get much schooling. Beatrice, however, was fortunate that her mother's father was a teacher. He encouraged the children, including the girls in the family, to get an education.

Many years later, Beatrice Lei explained that while growing up she had seen the medical needs of her ten brothers and sisters, and, as a result, she had become interested in medicine. There was no local doctor, but she did have an older brother who became a self-taught healer. When any of the children got sick, they would travel to see him for the medicines he would prescribe. However, Beatrice wanted more formal medical training and thanks to the work of a remarkable woman physician, Mary Hannah Fulton, it was available at a medical college for women in the provincial capital, Canton.

Dr. Fulton, a native of Ohio, had trained at Women's Medical College of Pennsylvania. After graduating in 1884, she had set out for south China, where an older brother, a missionary, was already working. In 1902 in Canton after she had already opened a hospital for women and children as well as a school for nursing, she began the Hackett Medical College for Women. Not only did she raise the money for this new institution, she even translated medical books into Cantonese for her students.

In 1927 Beatrice entered Hackett Medical College for a four-year medical course. In 1932, after she received her medical degree, the brand-new physician headed for Shanghai for a three-year residency in obstetrics and gynecology. Upon completion, she returned to her birthplace and to her family in Shantou to practice.

Dr. Lei, disturbed by the prevalence of tuberculosis in Shantou, was frustrated by her inability to do more for her patients. An American physician there told her about new, more effective treatments being used in San Francisco, and she decided to go to the United States to study them. She found a temporary position at San Francisco Children's Hospital, planning to return to China with new knowledge to help combat the disease.

However, when she completed her studies, it was 1939, and China had been invaded by Japan two years earlier. Japan had seized Shantou and the area around it. Returning home was out of the question.* She would have to remain in the United States. Since Dr. Lei's medical degree was not recognized in America, she supported herself working as a medical assistant in several hospitals in Richmond. It was still the Depression and at first the only jobs she could find paid no salary, just room and board. Eventually her qualifications were more appreciated and she worked her way up to a salary of sixty dollars a month, although out of that she had to pay for food and lodging.

During this time, Beatrice married Henry Lei, who had come to the United States after graduating from Peking (today Beijing) University with a degree in journalism. He had decided on a career in investments and real estate, and the two of them bought a small home in Oakland.+

A doctor she had met while working at a Richmond hospital encouraged her to take the California Medical Boards so she could be certified to practice as a physician. Successfully passing the Medical Boards not only made her work more professionally satisfying, it improved her earning power significantly.

In 1944, while Dr. Lei was working at the San Mateo Community Hospital, she received a call from Richard Moore, a physician with the Permanente Health Plan.

---
*After the war, Dr. Lei was relieved to find out that her family had survived the war by hiding in several rural villages.
+ It was at this time that her colleagues added an "e" to her family name in order to help themselves with its pronunciation.

Moore, an orthopedist, had been working with Garfield since the Grand Coulee days. Now one of the leaders of the shipyard medical group, Moore was also one of its most vigorous recruiters. He asked Dr. Lei if she would be interested in joining the group in taking care of shipyard workers. She recalled, "I told Dr. Moore that I was happy where I was, but he insisted that I come out to the facility and take a look. When I did, I liked what I saw and stayed." And stay she did, remaining in Richmond for thirty-two years, until her retirement in 1975.

In Richmond, Lei kept very busy caring for shipyard workers. It seemed to her that those from the Eastern states were not used to the cold, damp weather and many took sick. She later told her niece that when she looked back at that period of her life, it seemed to her that the work never stopped.

After the war came to an end, the shipyards closed, almost abruptly, and membership plummeted. Many physicians left to return to their fee-for-service practices. However, a core group, committed to the concept of prepaid group practice, remained. Dr. Lei was one of them. "Our staff dwindled to three doctors. Many of our doctors left the program and started private practice. Some of them asked me to join them, but I refused. There was still a need here [in Richmond]. Besides that, I wanted to continue practicing in Richmond. I have always liked the people who live and work here; Richmond has always been like home to me."

Not long after the formation of the Permanente Medical Group in 1948, Dr. Lei was invited to join as a partner. Although there had been a number of women on the medical staff during the war, she was the first to be offered a partnership in the new medical group, making her not only the first woman but the first Asian to hold such a position.

According to her niece, Dr. Lei never mentioned having had any special problems based on gender or ethnicity, although she always felt that her English was not as good as she would have liked. Even so, she developed very close relationships with many of her patients due to the personalized care that she provided. Every night, she made it a point to call her patients to see how they were doing. This care was much appreciated, and sometimes even after a child had graduated from college, a parent would bring her back to see Dr. Lei because of the almost familial feeling in the relationship.

After her retirement in 1975 at age sixty-five, she continued to take care of friends and family. Although Dr. Lei and Henry never had children of their own, her family knew that she felt very satisfied with her life. The children whose lives she had entered and helped, including the children in Richmond and the children in China, were a great source of personal satisfaction for her. She liked to say: "They are all my children."

Like her grandfather in China who had encouraged her to get an education, Dr. Lei helped her family's children go to college with both emotional and financial encouragement. She would often remind them of something she believed wholeheartedly: "Only knowledge can give your life meaning."

The Permanente Health Plan Gets National Attention
for the First Time

Paul de Kruif was a larger-than-life, hard-drinking, impulsive idealist and a friend to many of the major figures of the 1930s, '40s and '50s. He was a microbiologist who had been fired for criticizing the petty politics inside the internationally-respected medical research center where he had worked. He had begun a writing career as a way to replace his lost income and had become a best-selling author of nonfiction. He was also the co-writer, with Sinclair Lewis, of a highly regarded and popular novel, *Arrowsmith*. DeKruif's name never appeared as co-author, but it was one of his best-known works. Among the several generations of students inspired by that novel to enter careers in medicine many were Permanente physicians. Under his own name, de Kruif wrote books that prompted thousands of others into careers in medical research. He was also the first person to present the Permanente Health Plan to a national audience.*

In the May 1943 issue of *Reader's Digest*, Paul de Kruif published a perceptive article entitled, "Tomorrow's Health Plan Today." Those four pages, which he later expanded into a book, *Kaiser Wakes the Doctors*, show how quickly he had grasped what made the new health plan unique. In his florid but powerful style, he told millions of readers all about it. In so doing, he became the first high-profile individual

---

* It was the well-known physician Morris Fishbein who introduced de Kruif and Lewis. Ironically, it would be Fishbein who would later lead the American Medical Association's attack on the Health Plan while de Kruif became its earliest and most outspoken independent advocate.

to rise to the defense of the young health care program already under attack by people in the medical establishment who saw Henry Kaiser and "his" medical care program as a threat to their economic well-being.

In retrospect it seems inevitable that Henry Kaiser, Sidney Garfield, and Paul de Kruif would meet. It was only a question of when and where. Years before, de Kruif had been doing valuable work at the Rockefeller Institute studying the mechanisms of lung infections but had become disenchanted with what he saw as the wasteful internal politics of research. That, combined with what today would be called a midlife crisis, led him to walk away from his job, his wife and two sons he was not to see again for almost a quarter of a century. Now without a job, he started on a new career, writing. His first major assignment was to pair up with one of America's greatest writers, Sinclair Lewis, to create one of the best medical novels of all time, *Arrowsmith*. The original idea had been that Lewis would write the story and de Kruif would help with scientific detail. His expertise would provide accuracy as well as texture to the story of a young idealist who goes to work in one of the great research institutions only to discover that scientists there struggle for more than pure knowledge; they also become involved in petty infighting for fame and money. It wasn't long before the drafts of Lewis' novel started to read more like de Kruif's autobiography. Lewis wrote to his publisher, "There's a question as to whether he [de Kruif] won't have contributed more than I shall have." However, the realities of book publishing dictated that in 1925 the book appeared as the work of the already well-known Sinclair Lewis with "technical assistance" from Dr. Paul de Kruif.

Although De Kruif had received little recognition for his contribution to *Arrowsmith*, he more than made up for it with *Microbe Hunters* the next year. In this nonfiction book, the lives of science giants such as Leeuwenhoek, Pasteur, Koch, and other great figures in medical history, became gripping, vivid adventures. De Kruif told their stories using invented dialogue, but it carried the flavor of an exciting reality. He wrote about their weaknesses as well as their strengths so they were not just great; they became human. In his hands, dry scientific history became a detective story filled with fascinating characters. He had invented a new literary genre of science writing.

Seventy-five years later, *Microbe Hunters* is still in print. It has been translated into eighteen languages, spawned a Broadway play as well as a Hollywood movie, and turned Dr. de Kruif into a literary celebrity. Eventually, he published thirteen books and wrote more than two hundred articles for some of the most popular magazines of the day, particularly *Reader's Digest*. His exciting, easy-to-understand explanations of medical progress helped people appreciate the scientific advances being made in the 1920s, '30s and '40s. However, de Kruif, an idealist with strong convictions, was well aware of a darker side of medical progress. Physicians could do more and more for their patients, but fewer and fewer patients could afford the increased costs of the improved medical care. De Kruif took on this problem, for better or worse, the same way he took on every other problem—head-on.

He became excited by the ideas of the U.S. Surgeon General, Dr. Thomas Parran, and of Dr. C.C. Young, who were both convinced that the answer to at least part of the problem was preventive care. In December 1939, de Kruif arranged a luncheon for himself with President Roosevelt. He carried with him to the White House a carefully composed, two-page memo that proposed something radical: the establishment of a national, preventive health care program. There was a model for it; Dr. Young had already built a successful program in Michigan, paid in large part by the savings preventive care had made possible. The plan had earned the support of physicians familiar with it, and they believed that organized medicine would support a national version, since it didn't involve changing the fee-for-service payment system. Also, the chairman of the Federal Reserve Board had endorsed the economics of the idea, and Harry Hopkins, political adviser to FDR, had given it his blessing. The ducks were all in line. De Kruif headed for his meeting with FDR with a great deal of hope.

During his lunch with the President, de Kruif stressed that the one-hundred-million-dollar-a-year government investment would more than pay for itself and would alleviate a great deal of human misery. He compared it to investments being made at the time in huge, important public works projects such as dams. That afternoon, two years before Pearl Harbor, FDR replied that there was no money available. It was all going to be needed for tanks, planes, and bombs for a war that was on the horizon. (The President did say he personally supported efforts of a group of Washington, D.C. physicians to establish a prepaid health plan, despite efforts of the American Medical Association to stifle it.) The reference to public works projects, however, reminded FDR of Grand Coulee Dam, and he spent the rest of the luncheon talking enthusiastically about his plans for the Grand Coulee area. De Kruif couldn't bring the topic back to the preventive care proposal. By ignoring it, the President had rejected it. De Kruif was deeply disappointed.

Fast-forward three years, 1942, again in Washington, D.C., Henry Kaiser is there to testify before a congressional committee that is trying to balance the need for physicians on the home front versus the military. De Kruif is also there in his role of crusader, testifying against the government's Procurement and Assignment Service, which he says is abusing its power to draft physicians, using it to punish those doctors who break with mainstream medicine's conservative social values. At the hearings, he meets Henry Kaiser.

The more de Kruif hears about the shipyard medical program, the more fascinated he becomes. Here is a program that is actually putting into practice many of the principles de Kruif already believes in. A few days later de Kruif is on a train to California to see the Permanente Health Plan in operation for himself.

What he found in Oakland and Richmond exceeded his expectations. His *Reader's Digest* article, "Tomorrow's Health Plan Today," was an enthusiastic endorsement of the vision of Henry Kaiser and Sidney Garfield. Millions of people in the United States, as well as the readers of the British, Spanish, Portuguese, Swedish, and Chinese editions around the world, learned about the Permanente Health Plan through de Kruif's phrases: "the Kaiser Plan is really the Hippocratic Oath in action"; it is "a model of disease-fighting efficiency"; "the Mayo Clinic for the common man"; "no one delays going to a doctor because he 'can't afford' it"; and "the health pageant now unfolding in California is merely the opening scene in the epic program that will be written by industry and communities all over the United States collaborating wholeheartedly in the prepaid fight against disease and death."

Encouraged by interest in the article, de Kruif expanded the four pages into a book, *Kaiser Wakes the Doctors*, published in the United States and in England. Suddenly, thanks to the writing of Paul de Kruif, the emergency shipyard health plan was thrust into national and international prominence. Some would find great hope in the new model. Others would see a great threat. The fight was on. Several generations of doctors, politicians, and planners would be caught up in it. Nearly seven decades later, the battle over how health care in the United States should be organized and paid for still rages.

Henry Kaiser's *Inspiration*

According to Henry Kaiser, the untimely death of his fifty-two-year-old mother Maria in 1899 was due entirely to a lack of accessible medical care. HJK was fond of telling the story of how, when he was sixteen years old, she had died in his arms. In speeches and interviews he often related how her death had been the impetus for his commitment to the ideals of the Kaiser Permanente Health Plan. Although the details of the story, such as whether or not she had literally died in his arms, are open to question, there's no doubt that Kaiser himself came to wholeheartedly believe the story in all its details. There was an element of powerful, personal dedication on his part to the health plan. Perhaps he saw in the success of the Kaiser medical care program a living tribute to his mother, to whom he had been very close.

Several years ago, on a research trip to Kaiser-related sites around the United States I decided to try to locate the grave of Maria Kaiser, the woman who had inspired in her son such enthusiasm for a health care system that would make health care accessible and affordable to millions of Americans.

In 1889, when Henry Kaiser was seven, his parents Franz and Maria moved the family from his birthplace in Canojohairie, New York, forty-five miles west along the Erie Canal to Whitesboro, near Utica. By this time the family was becoming more Americanized; Franz became "Frank" and Maria was known to her new friends as Mary. After ten years in Whitesboro, she was taken sick. On December 1, 1899, she passed away, and, according to HJK biographer Albert Heiner, she had been buried in the Grandview Cemetery in Whitesboro.

Finding Grandview Cemetery was a bit more difficult than I had expected. Because Whitesboro has grown so much in the past few decades, the people I asked for directions were unsure exactly where the old cemetery was. I had visualized Grandview to be a small churchyard-style burial ground, but it turned out to be a three- or four-acre cemetery spread over some small hills. Once on the edge of Whitesboro, the cemetery was now surrounded by one- and two-family wood frame houses that look as though they had been built in the years immediately after World War II. Next to the graveyard's iron entrance gate is a small concrete building, probably an office of some sort, but clearly not in use. With no one to ask about the location of a Kaiser family grave, it would have taken days to find an individual marker; I knew I needed some help. I went back to the business area of Whitesboro and found the City Assessor's Office, where staff were able to tell me who owned the cemetery and even put me in touch with the caretaker by calling him at home.

"I think there is a Kaiser buried there but there's no stone." The caretaker's voice sounded very sure of the information he was passing on to me. He went on, "Let me look at my index cards and see what I can tell you."

All was quiet for several minutes until he'd found what he was looking for. "Yes, here it is, Francis Kaiser. Died in 1929. There's no stone. And the card doesn't say who paid for the plot."

It seemed very likely that this Francis was HJK's father, Franz. The date was right. Franz Kaiser had died in 1929. At the time of his death, he had been living with one of HJK's sisters and her husband in Daytona Beach, Florida. The two were operating what had been her brother's photographic business. They had bought HJK's stores in 1906 when Henry Kaiser had gone west to prove himself worthy of being given permission to marry Bess Fosburgh. Franz Kaiser's children must have wanted him buried in Whitesboro or, if she were in fact there, he may simply have wanted to be buried with his wife.

The cemetery record card apparently did give a general indication where Francis Kaiser was buried, and after a little pleading, the caretaker agreed to come out and meet me at the cemetery. When he showed me the section where Francis Kaiser was presumably buried, I knew I still had a lot of searching to do. He had only narrowed it down to about an acre stretching across two small hills. The caretaker shrugged; it was the best he could do and so left me to my task.

Henry Kaiser's parents gravesite in Whitesboro, New York. HJK often spoke of how the untimely death of his mother, because of the lack of medical care, was a constant inspiration to him to help improve and expand the Kaiser Permanente medial care program.

Persistence paid off. Contrary to what the sexton believed, it turned out that there was a Francis Kaiser gravestone. I was very pleased to see that it also marked the final resting place of Mary Kaiser, the woman Henry Kaiser called the inspiration for Kaiser Permanente. A small, barely legible, and slightly ironic, inscription on the side of the almost-forgotten Kaiser stone marker reads, "Perpetual Care."

Celebrating a Medical Center's Anniversary

The rapid growth of defense industries on the West Coast following the attack on Pearl Harbor in December 1941 set off one of the largest migrations in American history. Tens of thousands of Americans who had struggled through the Depression years flooded into the states of Washington, Oregon, and California, anxious to fill a need for labor that had outgrown the local labor pool. Each individual had his or her own story. To find a "typical" one would be impossible. A few years ago, someone told me about a Kaiser member with an unusually low Kaiser Permanente medical record number. From that number, I could tell that he had first joined during the shipyard days. I called him at home and asked if I could talk with him about his days in the shipyards and any experience he might have had with the medical care program there.

His story began on an African American sharecropper's farm in Texas seventy-five years before. It culminated in 2005 at a sixtieth-anniversary celebration of the Kaiser Permanente Health Plan.

Beginnings in Texas

Alfonzo Smith was born in Texarkana, Texas, on the northeast shoulder of the Lone Star State, near where Texas meets Oklahoma and Arkansas. His mother and father both died before he was old enough to have any memories of them. He was sent to live on a farm sharecropped by his grandparents. There they grew cotton, cultivated a garden for vegetables, and raised and butchered their own hogs. It was a life made difficult by many uncertainties, not the least of which was weather and an undependable water supply. During summer droughts their well would often go dry. Then the crops would fail. They collected what little rainwater they could for drinking from the runoff of their roof. But they managed to hold on. Any profit from the sale of crops, went to the general store to pay for supplies and seed the storekeeper had advanced them during the year. It was impossible to get enough ahead to have any sense of security.

When Smith was about ten years old, he was playing on his grandfather's mule wagon. He ran out on the narrow tongue of the wagon and slipped down into the traces. As he fell, he gashed his leg on a piece of steel used to hold the mules in place, ripping a chunk of flesh from the leg.

The ugly wound would not heal, but seeing a doctor was out of the question. People there, particularly African Americans, did not call doctors. Even if they could afford the fee, there were no doctors around. His grandmother, though, was well-versed in folk remedies. She made poultices, but the wound ulcerated. The young boy was in constant pain, and it seemed as though nothing could be done for him.

By the time he was thirteen, still suffering from the wound on his leg, Smith was thoroughly dissatisfied with life on his grandparents' farm. He ran off to live with an uncle in a small town in the Texas hill country. The uncle got him a job in a sawmill, fueling the steam furnaces that ran the plant with sawdust he would shovel in by the ton, often seven days a week. It was a particularly hellish job during the Texas summers. Always, he had to bandage his leg to keep it clean and always he had to live with the pain. Even so, he had a job at a time when many were desperate for any kind of work. He stayed for almost ten years before deciding to start a new life by heading off to Fort Worth to clear land for the expansion of Meacham Field, the city's municipal airport.

Before long, restlessness and curiosity got the better of Smith, and sometime around early 1940 he left Fort Worth and joined what was already a growing flow of emigrants from those parts of America with high unemployment to the "Golden State" of California, where the promise of jobs beckoned. Inevitably, because of the times and his age, he was notified to report to his draft board. Although he had been doing heavy work for more than ten years, when the Army gave him a physical, one look at the ulcer on his leg classified him as 4-F, the lowest rating. He was judged totally unfit for military service.

Industry was less fussy, though, and he was able to get a job on a railroad track maintenance crew, working for the Western Pacific Railway in the Sacramento area. Smith likes to point out that times were so hard back then that before he began working for Western Pacific, he'd never seen a paper dollar. His crew replaced wooden ties and worn-out rails and reinforced the ballast rock supporting the rails that carried the heavy loads of train traffic. Despite his weakened leg and the pain, even during the hot Central Valley summer, he was considered a good worker. Few knew about the constant throbbing from the ulcer he kept hidden under homemade bandages.

As the trains rushed by his work crew, Smith saw the tempo of war beginning to speed up. "That's when they was picking up the Japanese and sending them to camps. And that was a sad day, too, for me. . . . I saw it happen. They herded them in like they was herding cattle; worse. And some of those dear elderly people had been here for years. . . . They was crying and the screaming."

Cooler weather and the chance for better pay drew Smith to the Bay Area. He had heard that the Kaiser shipyards were hiring and that African Americans could get jobs there. Again, no one questioned him about his overall health. They needed workers and they just signed him up. No one knew about the ulcer on his leg.

The Health Plan in Action

After Smith had established himself in his new job on a clean-up crew in Yard No. 2, he decided to see if the Permanente Health Plan could do anything for his ulcerated leg. "I went to the Richmond hospital [the Permanente Field Hospital]. They didn't have anyone there that could take care of the situation, so they said, 'We'll send you to the Oakland hospital.'" He was referred to a dermatologist who then referred him to a surgeon. He remembered that this was first time he had ever been alone in a room with a white man. By this time the ulcer was about an inch-and-a-half long, "big enough for me to get my thumb in." Smith remembers that the surgeon looked at his leg and said, "Oh, well, yes, we'll take care of that. You come back and we'll do it."

"My eyes opened wide, wide, wide, after he said he could take care of it, because it had been so long, it had been a problem for a long time. . . . He did a vein strip, I guess what you might call it. He cut here in the groin, and he cut three strips here, and he cut here and he cut down here. It was numb but I could feel the kind of stripping of that." With the newly-improved blood supply, the ulcer that had not healed in all those years soon vanished. He was absolutely delighted.

I asked Mr. Smith if he remembered the name of the doctor who had done the surgery. Without the slightest hesitation he answered, "Dr. Grant." When I expressed surprise that he remembered the name so readily, Mr. Smith explained, "The reason why I don't have any problem—because he was such a wonderful person. I had never really seen a white person that great to a black person."

One thing Mr. Smith regretted was that he had never had the opportunity to tell Dr. Grant how much he appreciated the treatment he had received and what a difference it had made in his life.

An Emotional Reunion

By chance, not long before, for the Permanente Medical Group, I'd done an oral history with Dr. Grant and knew how to get in touch with him. So in late September in a park across from the Kaiser Oakland Medical Center, in a large tent filled with music, good food, and a crowd of past and present Kaiser Permanente employees celebrating sixty years of medical care, the two men were reunited. They hugged and laughed together as they looked at photos of the original hospital. "Your office was right there," said Mr. Smith, pointing to a window on the first floor.

An emotional reunion. A patient (Alonzo Smith, left) has the opportunity to thank the physician (Donald Grant, right) who changed his life.

"You're right," said Dr. Grant, smiling broadly, "that was it."

Another Permanente physician standing nearby said incredulously, "You can remember where your office was?"

"I ought to. I was there for forty years."

Meeting again brought up so many pleasant memories for both men that they found themselves holding on to each other's hands as they reminisced about their shared experiences nearly sixty years before. At that time, Dr. Sidney Garfield had just founded the medical care program and was determined to make the care as personal as possible. The story of Donald Grant and Al Smith is an indication that he had succeeded.

Acknowledgments

One of the most misleading things about the cover of a book is that it often has only one or two names on it, giving the impression that only the author(s) were responsible for the volume. But anyone who has been near the publishing world knows how untrue this is. On the list of people whose individual contributions fall between valuable and indispensable, I would start with Lois Boyle and the Richmond (California) Museum Association which she heads. It was Lois who originally suggested reshaping the shipyard columns I wrote for the Kaiser Permanente website and for various historical publications and putting them into book form. Sandi Genser Maack and Lynn Maack began the process of putting this book together by helping in the selection and organization of articles. Maria Sakovich, went well beyond her role of editor and was an immense help as both content and style editor as well as selector of many of the illustrations. Finally, but certainly not least, my thanks to Kiersten Hanna who, with what sometimes seemed like magic, but was the result of her professional skills and her enthusiasm, put words and pictures together in a way that enhanced both greatly.

Most of the photographs in this book came from the valuable collections of the Richmond Museum of History, maintained by Inna Soiguine, and the archives of Kaiser Permanente kept by their Heritage Resources Department. Others came from my collection and from issues of *Fore 'N' Aft* (the weekly publication of the Kaiser Richmond Shipyards). I also obtained photographs from the FDR Presidential Library in Hyde Park, New York, and the U.S. Army Medical Department, Office of Medical

History. Individuals and families were kind enough to allow use of photographs: Tom Debley, the Lei family, and the Green family. I also procured images from several internet sites: www.lovevinylrecordscom, www.aadl.org, and www.pa59ers.com, to name a few, and from the cover of *Modern Medicine* (Dec 1968).

About the Author
Steve Gilford

As far back into his childhood as he can remember, Steve Gilford enjoyed talking with his and his friends' parents and grandparents about their histories. Later, as a writer and producer of award-winning network television documentaries and radio news programs, he had the opportunity to interview literally hundreds of people from all sorts of backgrounds, including Nobel Laureates, whom he accompanied to Stockholm for a documentary about their research, and a cafe owner in a remote desert town in Utah for a peripatetic radio series. Twenty-five years ago, when his work as an independent writer and historian brought him to the former Kaiser Shipyards, he became fascinated with the story of how this place, in a few short years, went from marshland to the most productive shipyards in the history of the world and he began seeking out the people who made it happen.

www.ingramcontent.com/pod-product-compliance
Lightning Source LLC
Chambersburg PA
CBHW081219170426
43198CB00017B/2661